CW00520620

A Haunting at Farrar

Copyright © 2019 by Richard Estep & E. E. Bensen
All rights reserved. No part of this publication may be reproduced, distributed, or broadcast in any form, including photocopying, recording, or other electronic or mechanical methods, without the prior written permission of the authors, except in the case of short quotations contained within critical reviews and specific noncommercial uses as dictated by fair use doctrine under United States copyright law.

A Haunting at Farrar

Investigating One of the World's Most Haunted Schools

Richard Estep & E. E. Bensen

For Nancy & Jim

Thanks for sharing the schoolhouse with us.

Foreword

John E.L. Tenney

When I was thirteen years old, I started skipping school. I loved learning, but I found that the traditional "learning environment" starved my quest for information more than it could have ever fed it. Since I was unfamiliar with what a person was supposed to do when they skipped school, I did what I thought I was supposed to do... I went to the local library and read about subjects I found interesting. I inhaled books on mythology, religion, and folklore. Some days I would spend five or six hours in the newspaper archive scanning through what seemed to be endless newspapers while looking for reports of haunted houses, monsters, and unidentified flying objects. School seemed like the last place I would ever want to go to learn anything.

As I grew older and started attending college, I couldn't help but feel that although I had "chosen" my classes, I was still being stifled. Professors told me what I should and shouldn't be writing about or studying. My ideas and outspokenness brought me to a breaking point. Luckily for me, it was at this time I was offered a job working as a researcher for a major television show. I took the job and once again "skipped school". At this point, nearing my mid-twenties, I was fully convinced that there was nothing to be gained, (for me) by going to school.

Time passed.

In 2013 I was invited to attend an event at Farrar school in Iowa. I loaded up my car and drove out there, not only to meet with my fellow weirdos, but to investigate a location of which I had no preconceived ideas. I knew nothing about Farrar. Its legends and history were a blank slate to me, and this made visiting the school one of the situations I truly love. For me, there is nothing more exciting than walking into an allegedly haunted location and having absolutely no distorted notions about the place. I can let the location and surrounding environment be what it is, without bias.

Farrar flummoxed me, and in doing so, I fell in love with it. It was quiet and loud, inactive and hyperactive. It was cold and hot and warm and spoke and sang and laughed all while standing mute. Lockers slammed, ethereal footsteps ran down hallways, and yet, for all of the multitude of experiences and non-experiences, the one thing I came to learn was that this school could teach me something. For the first time in my life, school became a place to learn.

A year after my first visit to Farrar I had begun work on the television show *Ghost Stalkers*. One of the tasks we had set for ourselves in the show was going to locations that had never been shown on television. Due to the number of locations featured on countless TV programs before ours, this in itself was a monumental project. I suggested Farrar for our final episode.

When anyone watches a TV show, they are only seeing random slices of the overall investigation. One hour of television could never capture what Farrar offers of itself. The situations I encountered during filming were instrumental in the evolution of my thoughts about the experiences of Life, Death and if there is something more. The surrounding community and the people who care for Farrar are also essential components in the seemingly participatory nature of the place. What you take from and give to Farrar is as important as what it gives and takes from you.

If you allow yourself to experience Farrar, then you are literally taking yourself back to school. There are lessons to be learned and, if you are willing, you will become a more informed student of what seems to be the very strange reality we are existing within.

It is not lost on me that the final shot of the last episode of *Ghost Stalkers* is of me and my co-investigator Chad Lindberg, sitting in a classroom, discussing the psychical researchers who came before us. We end the show by beginning a dialog about the nature of "ghosts". We are the living students, who will someday be dead, discussing the dead, who were once the living, that have become the teachers. Back and forth, around and around. We are never done learning. The more you know the more you realize you don't know. That every 'answer' leads to another question, is one of the many lessons you learn at Farrar.

As someone who always dreaded going to school, it could only be Farrar which would shape me into a person that tells other people... *go to school.*

Farrar is waiting to teach us and we have much to learn.

John E.L. Tenney

Introduction

E. E. Bensen

I had never heard of the Farrar Elementary School until sitting at home one day while taking in the final of six episodes of the television show, *Ghost Stalkers*.

While the series received overall mixed reviews, as is the case with nearly every show in the genre, for my tastes, it remains to be one of the best paranormal shows ever produced. I simply like the format.

There are only two investigators, and each one explores a location solo on consecutive nights, while the other one stands watch via stationary cameras in an RV outside, maintaining very little contact. My favorite aspect of the show is the actual investigators themselves. On the one hand, we have John Tenney, a seasoned paranormal researcher with a good sense of humor, and a formidable resume in the field.

On the other, we have Chad Lindberg, an actor and budding paranormal enthusiast and investigator. Most of his time on screen was spent being scared to death, and it showed.

I enjoyed seeing this, because it was a genuine reaction and a reminder that what we do as paranormal investigators is really not all that normal. It is easy to become jaded after you have numerous investigations under your belt, so it was fun to see Chad roam some very deserted and haunted locations and react to his experiences. He comes across as a very likeable guy as well.

The show focused on the concept of "portals," which was an interesting choice to me. In simplistic terms, a portal is thought to be a point at which the physical world and supernatural world intersect, thus allowing paranormal entities to cross into our reality.

Exactly why or how these would form, or if they even exist, is a topic of debate. In extremely haunted locations, are portals created when tragic or violent events somehow tear a hole in space-time, thus forming this gateway? Who knows for sure, and personally I am on the fence about whether there is such a thing, but I'll take the *MythBusters* approach and simply call it "plausible."

The final episode of the series was filmed at Farrar, and it proved to be very interesting. The investigators had multiple run-ins with a large, shadowy figure that has been nicknamed "the Principal."

In our research for this book, I have come to think that few people actually believe this entity to be a former principal of the school, but rather it is simply a fitting name, given the nature of the thing, and of the location in which it is found.

In all cases, this shadow entity was observed to be, for lack of a better term, stalking the investigators. I found this to be true in my own investigations of Farrar in later years. I'll elaborate on that shortly.

One of the more compelling situations that John Tenney was involved in, was that of his audio recorder being seemingly disabled by the schoolhouse, or by an entity within its walls. He would attempt to speak into the recorder, and find only static on the playback. However, after stepping just outside the front door of the building, the recorder worked just fine. He tested this multiple times, always with the same result. I found this to be utterly fascinating. Over the years we have had many instances of unexplainable battery drain during investigations, and one time, at the Museum of Colorado Prisons, we actually had multiple pieces of equipment get "fried" simultaneously by some unseen force.

I'd like to share with you now, a brief history of my past experiences with the Farrar school prior to the investigation that led to co-authoring this book. My interest in all things paranormal spans back to some weird experiences that I had as a child.

I spent many years reading books and watching television shows and documentaries, then later on, taking in stories and research via the internet. I also spent a fair amount of time experimenting with EVP (Electronic Voice Phenomena) in the early 2000s, and for about a decade after. Eventually, I decided to expand my search for the unknown, and began dabbling with various paranormal groups nearly ten years ago. I have done numerous field investigations of both famous and obscure reportedly-haunted locations, and I have experienced many utterly unexplainable things. These days, I investigate with a group known as AAPI (American Association of Paranormal Investigators). I spent a fair amount of time in my first book detailing my involvement in the field, and my experiences, so I will not take up more paragraphs here on such things. Instead, let us continue talking about Farrar.

During a trip-planning session in late 2015, AAPI went through a long list of possible investigation locations. Farrar had piqued my interest via the *Ghost Stalkers* TV show, so I suggested it to the others, and we quickly adopted the idea of visiting the school in March of 2016 for a few nights of investigation.

As we set out on the nine-hour drive from our home in Denver, Colorado, I turned on an audiobook to keep us entertained.

I'm afraid to report that the drive from where I live to Iowa is about as unengaging as possible. It is pretty much a collection of truck stops and farms, a real snoozer, especially if you're the one behind the wheel. The audiobook was called *A Funny Thing Happened on the Way to Heaven,* by Corey Taylor. Hailing from Iowa, and in addition to having a keen interest in the paranormal, Corey is also a member of the popular bands Slipknot and Stone Sour.

While listening to the book, we were surprised and quite pleased when the topic of Farrar came up. I had no idea that it was a part of the book, but Corey had stories to tell, and we were certainly eager to listen. This was not to be the first instance of the school coming up randomly in unexpected ways. In July of 2016, between our first and second visits, we attended a screening of the documentary film *Sir Noface* by Chad Calek.

The film is centered on some video footage of an apparition collected by a team out of Australia called West Sydney Paranormal Research, or WSPR for short. Included in the documentary is video of a strange light phenomenon that the team encountered regularly, and could sometimes get to happen on demand. As the story goes, a certain entity, or entities maybe, on Cockatoo Island could literally cause a blackened room to light up for an instant. On film, it looked somewhat like a camera flash had gone off in the dark, but those present insist that it was indeed paranormal in nature, and even go so far as to say that it produced no shadows.

At the film screening, I had a chance to meet both Chad Calek and the leader of WSPR, Craig Powell. I didn't know it until I saw him again face-to-face and shook his hand, but it turns out that I had actually met Craig during an event in Cripple Creek, Colorado, some months or maybe years earlier. We recognized each other immediately, and have loosely kept in touch ever since. As for the flashes of light, Chad indicates in the film that he has actually seen this phenomenon once before, at none other than the Farrar school in Iowa. Once again, the school sitting amongst the farm fields in rural Midwest America managed to weave its way into my consciousness.

The audiobook sufficiently passed the time in the car, and we arrived at the school late in the afternoon on Sunday, March 6, 2016. I recall standing in front of it, and staring up at the three- story building with anticipation. There was something about the place, but I couldn't put a finger on it, either then or now, for that matter. Paranormal investigators will often claim to be drawn to a certain location, and while this hasn't happened to me all that often, Farrar is one of those locations for me. I just want to hang out in there. I want to investigate it, and I want to experience it. I'm really not sure why, beyond the obvious reasons.

We were greeted warmly by owners Nancy and Jim Oliver, and treated to a tour by Nancy, who related some of her strange experiences in the building to us. We also got familiar with the building layout and the rules to access it during our two-day stay. I knew in my gut that something big was going to happen to me in there, and I just recall thinking, "This is going to be good." It turns out that I wasn't wrong, as the experience I had that night ranks as one of the top two I've ever had investigating the paranormal. That is saying a lot, actually, as I've spent countless hours doing it, and I've had some pretty incredible experiences, as documented in my books.

There is a large auditorium on the third floor of the building, which also happens to be considered the most haunted floor by the majority of visiting paranormal teams. On the first night, our group, totaling six people, spent a fair amount of time in there before opting to retreat to the space heater located in a break room on the first floor. It was very cold in the building, so we had to investigate in short bursts, and then go warm up for a while.

One thing that I immediately noticed about the school was that it can take on a very different feeling at night. In broad daylight, it is perfectly serene, and walking around in there alone is not a problem at all. In the darkness however, sometimes it feels like you are being followed by *something,* and the feeling is very distinct and intense. Chad Lindberg described it as "relentless" in the *Ghost Stalkers* episode. Normally I'd agree with most that would chalk this up to simply walking around an old empty building in the dark; however, I happen to have wandered around many buildings in that same scenario. I can confidently report that not all of them feel this way, and Farrar doesn't always either, for that matter. I'm convinced there is something to it, and I'd actually say that I proved it that night without a shadow of a doubt, incoming pun intended.

The other five investigators wandered out of the auditorium, and made a right turn to head down the stairs at the end of the hall. I walked out of the large room, and stopped in the middle of the hallway, still facing forward. The flashlight beams of my counterparts were aimed away from me, and danced on the walls, floor, and ceiling to my right. At this moment, I had an intense feeling that I was being watched from the left side. Turning my head in that direction, it was nearly pitch black at the end of the hall, where another stairway is located. For a few moments, I stared into the darkness, all but certain that something, or someone, was staring back.

I held a flashlight in my right hand, and slowly raised it up in front of my chest, across my body, then pressed the button to turn it on. There, at the end of the hallway and down several stairs, in the stairwell landing, was what looked like a black head and a shoulder leaning around the corner. I fixed my gaze on it, trying to work out what exactly it was. It just looked wrong, unnatural, and made little sense to be there at all. For a few seconds my brain played around with the image, trying to figure out how it could be my shadow, or that of one of the others, who were now almost entirely off the floor, down the hall to my right. Suddenly, it recoiled out of sight around the corner, faster than any mere mortal could possibly move, thus removing any doubt in my mind of what I had just witnessed. This rapid movement scared the proverbial crap out of me, if I'm being honest. My heart pounded as I stood there, illuminating a now empty hallway and stairway landing.

I turned and hurriedly walked to catch up with the others, looking over my shoulder several times, my mind racing due to what I had just seen. I've been fortunate to witness many "shadow figures" and other shadow-like phenomena in my paranormal adventures, but something that had never happened before was managing to catch one in a flashlight beam. Before that experience, if you had asked me whether it was possible, I'd have bet good money that it wasn't. I'd have asserted that it would probably disappear and be diffused by the light. Well, I can safely say that at least in some cases, it *is* possible. I can't really wrap my mind around the mechanics of this, other than to say that what I saw must have been physically manifested in some way. I saw absolutely no features, just a perfectly black silhouette. It made no sound, and was at least six feet tall. It also turned out that the corner it was leaning around was actually the closed stairwell door, meaning it was leaning *through* the door. This means that light couldn't penetrate it, but the wooden door seemed to have no problem. How very odd.

It was an extreme privilege to witness such a truly amazing and shocking thing. That it remained still and let me drink in the visual scene for a few seconds, is something that I will never forget. I don't think that it was trying to scare me, but instead was just extending a greeting of sorts. We stood there locked in a mutual gaze for a few seconds, and I felt no malicious intent from it whatsoever. These days, I can truthfully say that I have quite literally come face-to-face with a "ghost", thanks to Farrar. When I reflect back on my experiences pursuing this crazy field, I often think of this moment in particular. I knew that I would find something, given the things that happened to me as a kid, but I had no idea just how potent those experiences could actually be until many years later.

The first few chapters of this book detail a road trip that Richard Estep, Stephen Weidner, and I took from Denver to the Farrar Schoolhouse in Iowa. Richard and I have written our narratives about the events that took place separately, and we've included them here in their entirety. As is the case when you experience something with a friend, and then relay the events to another person, of course, there will be some overlap in the re-telling and possibly even some minor discrepancies, as people tend to remember varying small details in slightly different ways. We are certainly not immune to this, and it is our hope is that the reader will tolerate it, and find interest in the two different perspectives and means of storytelling presented here. The assumption is that it is better to read our firsthand accounts as they are, rather than to whitewash too many small discrepancies for fluidity purposes. In this way, you get the whole story as we collectively remember it. I will assure you that we both sought to tell the whole truth, and nothing but the truth. We also split interviewing duties with several people who have been kind enough to share their experiences at the school. Throughout this book, you'll see a heading with the name of the author at the beginning of each section.

Now, let's not be late for school, shall we? – E. E. B.

Chapter One

Day 1 - E. E. Bensen

Saturday, September 22, 2018. I woke up around seven o'clock in the morning and grabbed a quick shower, before loading paranormal investigating gear and a suitcase into the back of my SUV. The first stop was to pick up Stephen Weidner, founder of AAPI, and a very good friend of mine. There would be only three of us in total attending this supernatural adventure. We made our way to points north and arrived at fellow author Richard Estep's house between nine and ten in the morning. After a short visit with Richard's wife, Laura, his dog, and a black cat or three, we finished loading up the vehicle and headed east.

Our destination was Bellevue, Nebraska, and that night we would be investigating the Squirrel Cage Jail in Council Bluffs. The drive is 550 miles, and about seven and a half hours, give or take. We made our way across farmland USA, stopping only when necessary, as we knew that the timeline was pretty tight. The previous night, Richard had covered a shift as a paramedic, so we ended up setting out a little bit later than originally planned so he would have at least a small shot at getting some rest.

After checking-in to our hotel in Bellevue, we stopped at a Village Inn restaurant close by and quickly shoved down some dinner. At one point our waitress, who was probably fairly bored given the place was nearly empty, asked what we were doing that night. I hesitated for a moment, but a few years ago I had decided to always give a very straightforward answer to this question, because it generally elicits an amusing response. I looked at her, and stoically said something like, "Well, we are headed to Council Bluffs to do a paranormal investigation of the old jail." I then waited to see what her reaction would be.

The waitress was immediately enthralled with this idea, and proceeded to tell us that the Village Inn was also allegedly haunted. Throughout our meal, she would stop by briefly and ask more questions, while also sharing stories of various haunted places in the area. We appreciated this, and generally I love talking to people about this stuff, but frankly we were in a hurry.

Upon finishing our meals rapidly, in a scene that I can only describe as something similar to that which happens after a fresh kill occurs on the Serengeti, we paid our bill and headed back out to the vehicle. I pointed the navigation system at the Squirrel Cage Jail, and I will neither confirm nor deny the level of regard given to posted speed limit signs. Somehow, after travelling so far and having to do so much that day, we pulled into the parking area of the jail at the agreed upon time of precisely 8:00 in the evening.

We were greeted by the manager of the museum, Kat, whom we had met on a previous visit in October of 2017. Once again, she was very awesome to talk to, and gave us an excellent tour of the facility. The jail is a fascinating structure that is cylindrical in shape, and actually could rotate to load prisoners into cells three stories high. It most certainly would be a modern fire marshal's worst nightmare, however, as I could see no way to quickly unload occupants in the event of a fire. Today, the cell block is stationary and has not moved in many years, but Kat indicated to us that efforts are under way to see if it is possible to get it moving again. That would be pretty cool to see if they can figure it out.

We spent about five hours or so exploring the jail and

doing various paranormal investigation activities like EVP sessions, and using strange devices to attempt spirit communication, but overall things were very quiet. On our previous visit, we had gotten a few faint EVP responses on our audio recorders, and registered an anomalous stick figure on an SLS camera; during this visit, however, we were not to be rewarded with anything like that. Still, it was fun checking the place out again, as it is a very cool location indeed. We packed up our gear and headed back to the hotel for some well-earned rest. After all, we still had four days of investigation ahead of us.

Chapter Two
Day 2 - Richard Estep

Located close to the very center of the state of Iowa, the town of Farrar is a small, blink-and-you'll-miss-it sort of place. According to the public data records, Farrar has thirteen houses, one church… and an abandoned school.

"There she is," Erik said as we crested the rise of a small hill. "Farrar Elementary."

Our home for the next three nights was a three-story brick structure that looked rather imposing in the early afternoon sunlight.

A flagpole stood directly outside, though who knew the last time that Old Glory had been flown from it.

As we drove slowly up the long driveway, it became apparent that many of the windows were boarded up, which had the effect of making the place look even less inviting.

Yet it would be a mistake to think that nobody was looking after the place. Sloping grass lawns had been neatly trimmed, and there wasn't a piece of trash to be seen, other than inside a black wheeled trashcan that sat outside the school.

Three men were sitting casually in chairs outside the main doors. They watched us as Erik parked the car and we got out, introducing themselves as the owner, Jim, and the caretaker, Will. I already knew Jonah, a paranormal investigator that I had met through our shared fondness for Iowa's haunted Malvern Manor.

Handshakes were exchanged, and after a little small talk, Will kindly offered to show us around. Will is not a small man, but despite being gruff and no-nonsense, he is also extremely friendly, and I found myself warming to him immediately. As he spoke about the school and the land upon which it was built, it soon became very obvious that he had a deep and abiding fondness for the place. He really is the ideal caretaker for Farrar Elementary.

It was a beautiful September day, warm and sunny but not stiflingly hot. A gentle breeze rustled the branches and leaves. Will decided to start outside, leading us around the grounds and pointing out areas of interest.

Will has a long stride, and we three middle-aged paranormal investigators had to work hard to keep up with him. Our first stop was the north-west corner of the school, where a large tree stood. Its age has been estimated at 260 years.

During the filming of the TV show *Ghost Stalkers*, Will is heard to say that researcher David Rountree once told him that the tree was used as the focal point for celebratory ceremonies by the Native Americans. Several other visiting psychics, independently of one another, have told him that the tree exudes a mysterious form of energy.

During a public event, a researcher named Chris Sutton came out to Farrar. Chris, Will, and several other participants decided to try an experiment. The group all formed a circle around the tree, while Chris started drumming. It was a hot night, and everybody's clothes were soaked through with sweat, sticking to their bodies in awkward places. There wasn't even the slightest suggestion of a breeze. Mosquitoes swarmed around the experimenters, alighting on any stretch of exposed skin they could find, and eliciting a series of annoyed slaps and swats.

Chris increased the pace of his drumming, chanting along in time with the rhythm. Finally reaching a crescendo, he suddenly stopped and told those assembled to 'feel the energy.' No sooner had he spoken than a breeze came up out of nowhere, offering a few moments of welcome relief from the heat that was sapping everybody's strength.

Jonah had been one of the visiting investigators. He had been walking around the outside of the circle. Once he stepped foot inside it, the sense of raw energy became almost palpable.

"It was just *insane*," he said, thinking back to the events of that night and shaking his head. "There was some kind of connection. We could all feel it."

Placing his hand on the tree, Will confirmed that he, too, could sense the flow of energy that had been generated. He believes that the tree itself was calling out to him personally.

Part-way through telling this story, as the five of us were standing in the shade of that very same tree, Will suddenly reached out and slapped me on the forehead. My jaw dropped. What the heck had just happened?

"I've been wanting to do that to him for so long..." Stephen smirked.

"Sorry, man. Mosquito," Will explained, picking up his story without missing a beat. I reached up to touch my forehead and sure enough, my two fingertips came away coated with a tiny, bloody smear.

Picking up the narrative once more, Will told us that he and the tree then engaged in what can only be described as some kind of psychic conversation, with information passing back and forth between the two of them in a way that, Will says, is almost impossible for him to describe. It is important to emphasize that no drugs or hallucinogens were involved.

"What did the tree want?" I wondered.

"Two things," Will said. "It wanted me to tell its story, and it wanted to live on. One of the investigators had one of those spirit box things going, you know?"

I nodded. 'Spirit box' is a generic term used among members of the para-community for an electrical device which is believed by some to have the capacity for communicating with disembodied entities. Although Will did not hear it at the time, he would later hear that a voice from the spirit box had said, *Praise the tree.*

Will had then sunk to his knees, as if in prayer, and had begun to commune more deeply with the tree.

"At that moment, I felt myself get pulled down to my knees, and I was just *bawling*," Will recalled. "I could feel the essence of the tree itself, from the inside…"

(Author's note: Having seen the footage of the incident described by Will, I do not doubt that he underwent a deep and fulfilling experience that night. I do not, however, believe that the voice coming through the spirit box said the words PRAISE THE TREE, but it must be pointed out that this is just my opinion, and that such interpretations are always highly subjective. I invite the reader to judge for themselves and make up their own minds by viewing the video. It can be found at:

https://m.youtube.com/watch?v=p3vOzG6bEqY&t=296s).

A series of images began to flash through Will's brain, one following another at an immense rate of speed. Each was a mental picture of a different tree. At first, they seemed to be random and make no sense, but then Will realized that the images were all linked by a common thread. He and his son had worked as private contractors, and the pictures he was being shown all represented trees that they had both cut down as part of their job.

Ever since his experience with the Farrar Elementary School tree that night, he has lacked the stomach to ever cut down another tree. In fact, just a short time before our meeting, Will had been offered a contract to chop down a tree, and had actually managed to talk the prospective customer out of it…and in the process, cost himself close to two thousand dollars' worth of potential income.

I'm curious as to why Will thinks that Farrar Elementary is haunted. After all, when we delve down deep into the history of many hauntings, we find events that are often tragic and violent in nature, sources of extremely strong emotion which seem to be capable of imprinting themselves — or at least, some residue of themselves — onto the environment, to be picked up on by eyewitnesses at a future time. To the very best of our knowledge, Farrar has none of that. Its history is unspectacular, to say the least, untainted by tragedy as far as we can ascertain. So why, then, does the school seem to be so paranormally active?

"Hundreds of years' worth of changes, this land and this tree have seen," Will said, gazing off across the fields. "I think that we're dealing with the spirits of the land here. The school itself, well, that's just incidental. It ended up here, but the earth spirits were here long before that, and they'll be here long after it's gone."

Stopping to think about it, Will's theory made a great deal of sense. Unless there was some deep, dark mystery lurking in the elementary school's past, then there must be *some* other explanation for the haunting. There are no deaths on record at the location, or at least, none that the authors of this book could find. And while hauntings can also occur in places where there was a great deal of happiness and joy, such as homes, fire houses, and hotels, it is debatable whether a school would fit that description. While for some people, the old saying that 'your schooldays are the happiest days of your life' may be true, just as many people had a thoroughly miserable time at school and couldn't wait to escape.

But in addition to the everyday routine of classes and sports games, the school was also used for social functions. It was one of the few sizable venues for miles around that could host dances, soirees, and town hall meetings, among other things. It may be that concerts and wedding receptions also took place there, though at this time, that is conjecture.

Although he believes in the presence of a number of spirit portals that are said to reside within the school itself, allowing entities to pass back and forth from one plane of existence into our own and back again, it is Will's opinion that the crux of the Farrar haunting involves earth energy and elemental, native-type spirits.

"I'm proud to be the caretaker of this grand old place," he said, leading us back toward the front doors. "I like to see as many people as possible pass through these doors, just so they can experience the place for themselves."

"What's the best way to get results here?" I asked. We had three days and nights at Farrar, and I wanted to maximize our chances of gathering some evidence of the paranormal. Who better to ask than the caretaker?

"Well, you may not like this answer, but I think that your best bet is to shut everything off. Lights, cameras, recorders, everything like that. Then just sit quietly and experience it for yourself."

We had no way of knowing it at the time, but Will's suggestion would turn out to be uncannily accurate.

It was dark inside the school. Once the heavy front doors close behind you, it is like entering another world. The transition from bright sunlight to gloom and shadow was jarring, to say the least.

To the casual eye, Farrar Elementary looks like one of a thousand other American schools — and not that much different from the one I went to as a child in England. When the school closed for the final time in 2004, many of the fixtures and fittings were simply left in place.

Wandering the hallways, I saw the names of teachers affixed to the wall above classroom doors, and those of students written on lockers. Books still sit on shelves, along with the cards which indexed and cataloged them in the library. Educational posters cover the walls, maps of the world and instructions for performing CPR. In a way, the school was like a time capsule from fourteen years ago, frozen in stasis until such time as the building is either renovated... or demolished.

A musty smell pervades the entire building, the stale odor of decay that most old buildings have. Although the owners, and Will the caretaker, are all doing their best to keep the school clean and declutter it a little, they are fighting an uphill battle. Spiders are plentiful in the darker, danker areas, leaving cobwebs in their wake. If you are a paranormal investigator or enthusiast, however, you should *not* let this prevent you from visiting.

Will led our motley crew up to the third floor, where we found ourselves standing in a long hallway with open doorways leading to classrooms branching off on either side.

"This right here is *probably* going to be your most active area," he said, spreading his arms wide.

"What, the hallway?" I asked.

"No, the entire floor." He led us through one of the doorways into a very large room, one which he described as 'the auditorium.' The name was well-deserved. A large stage dominated one end, while the rest of it was just open space. I recognized the room from the episode of *Ghost Stalkers*, in which Chad Lindberg had taken to the stage and put on an impromptu one-man performance in an attempt to coax the spirits out. The only thing that occupied the stage now were a couple of old armchairs. As we would soon discover, they were surprisingly comfortable, and offered a commanding view of the entire room.

Stephen and Erik had been in the auditorium before, but to me it was new territory. I wandered around, poking into all of the corners and reading the leftover old posters that were still fixed to the walls and boards. I kept one ear on Will, who was telling us that this was his wife's favorite room, and now had become his favorite too — primarily because they had gotten married on the very same stage just a few years back. John Tenney, of *Ghost Stalkers,* officiated at the ceremony.

To my mind, this proved their love for Farrar Elementary like nothing else. I mean, just how enraptured with a haunted location did you have to be in order to get *married* there? (Says the man who got married on the grand mezzanine staircase of one of his favorite haunted hotels…)

Will was regaling us with the story of his wedding, when suddenly Jonah stiffened and moved out into the hallway. "Did you guys hear that?" We shook our heads, no. "I just heard a little girl scream."

I had been recording the entire time. When I played the audio file back afterward, no scream had been captured. It would have been easy to apply Ockham's Razor and assume that Jonah had simply been hearing things, or that the scream was nothing more than a product of his imagination, but as we would come to learn from personal experience, strange auditory phenomena which are heard by some but not by others are a fairly common experience at Farrar.

"*Hello*?" Will called out.

There was no response.

"That was rude, young lady," he said casually, apparently talking to thin air. "But fun. Very fun."

Obviously, little fazed Will on his home turf. He resumed the tour without missing a beat, launching into an anecdote about the night that he and his wife had come in to open up the schoolhouse prior to the arrival of visitors. Opening up was a relatively simple and straightforward process, one that primarily involved turning the water supply to the building back on, then rounding up all of the errant toys and placing them on the stage. This was something that they did because the spirits of the children tended to be most active on the stage.

Will and his wife, Jacquelyn, usually began at the top of the building and worked their way down, but this time, for whatever reason, they did things in reverse, starting downstairs and working their way up. By the time they reached the third floor, the sun had already gone down. Everything was dark and quiet up there.

He was carrying a puppet in his hand, having picked it up downstairs and brought it with him. While his wife waited at the foot of the stairs, Will carefully made his way up onto the stage. A small amount of ambient light filtered in from the outside through the windows, but even though his eyes were beginning to adjust to the darkness, he could still see little in the way of any real detail.

In fact, it was *too* dark — almost unnaturally so. Having been inside Farrar Elementary countless times after dark, Will knew the school inside and out, so much so that he could confidently walk around it with the lights out. But not this night. Something was *off*, for want of a better word.

He was getting disoriented, to the point that he accidentally walked into a wall without knowing that it was there.

"Honey, could you come up here, please?"

Somewhat reluctantly, Jacquelyn made her way slowly and carefully up onto the stage to join him. She has, as Will likes to put it, 'a way with the ghosts' at Farrar, and called out to them, asking them to show themselves to her.

Just as she made the request, Will happened to glance off to his right. There, sitting in one of the armchairs, was a whitish-grey figure. Jacquelyn saw it too — she described seeing the same figure, one that was clearly the size of a grown adult.

Reaching slowly into his pocket, the caretaker pulled out his lighter and flicked it on. In the light of the dancing flame, he could see that the chair was completely empty.

Ordinarily, it would be easy to dismiss this as a simple trick of the mind, or the eyes playing tricks. But Will and Jacquelyn both agreed on what they saw, as they saw it.

Shadow figure sightings are an extremely common occurrence at Farrar, particularly up on the third floor. Some witnesses claim to see adult-sized figures, whereas others report seeing children — especially on the stage in the auditorium.

"We've been told by psychics that there are two portals in the school," Will said. "One is located in the auditorium, the other in the principal's office. I don't think that we, as living people, are supposed to see those portals...those revolving doors. But that's what I think we got a glimpse of that night. I've seen a lot of strange things here, but I've never seen anything like THAT, either before or since."

We moved on a little further down the hallway. Things didn't feel so bad, but I had to remind myself that this was the afternoon. I could already tell that things would feel significantly different once night had fallen.

"Now we need to talk about the big guy," Will went on. "The shadow figure. You know, the one that Tenney reacted to in that episode of *Ghost Stalkers*. He drew a picture of what he saw."

Will advised us that once it got dark, one of us ought to sit on the steps leading up to the principal's office and just 'zone out,' focusing our eyes on infinity and gazing out along the length of the third-floor hallway.

"If you're lucky, you'll see him, coming up that staircase..."

This is the entity that has come to be nicknamed 'the Principal' by some, and 'the Janitor' by others. Erik remains convinced that this was the large shadow figure that he had encountered during an earlier visit to Farrar. It remains one of the most impressive paranormal events he has ever experienced, and has made a lasting impression on him that still lingers to this day.

There are several theories as to the identity of the Principal/Janitor. For his part, Will isn't overly fond of either moniker, pointing out that the school has had numerous principals and janitors over the years, and there is no concrete evidence to prove that this tall shadow man happens to be any one of them.

One night, Will and Jacquelyn were cleaning things up inside the school, when she remarked that the atmosphere felt unusually heavy. Jonah, who was hanging out with them, grew excited. He wanted to get out there and find out what the cause of the heaviness was.

While Jonah and Jacquelyn were doing their best to investigate, Will took a seat and began to zone out, gazing off into the darkness.

And there it was: a tall human shape, filling one of the doorways from top to bottom. Jacquelyn and Jonah were blissfully unaware of his presence. Will got slowly to his feet and walked toward the figure, being carefully not to move too quickly in case he managed to spook it somehow. Suddenly, with near-lightning speed, the shadow man lunged at Will, arms outstretched coming straight at him. The caretaker took a step back. The shadow man reversed direction, dashing downstairs and out of sight.

"What the hell was *that?*" Jonah wanted to know. He had seen the shadow figure going for Will, and stood there with his mouth open, hardly able to believe what his eyes were telling him. Will just laughed.

"It startled me, but it didn't *scare* me," Will explained. "You see, that's the difference between a paranormal investigator and a caretaker. A caretaker doesn't get to punch out and go home. You're always here, and it's in your face so often, you pretty much start to get used to it."

I was fascinated by the shadow man's behavior, and asked Will if he had gotten any sense of the entity's motivations. Was it deliberately trying to scare him, or was it simply a sense of curiosity at play? Will believes it is mostly the latter, though there was still a scare factor associated with it.

He had seen the tall shadow figure before, in other parts of the school. The two of them seem to have developed a kind of detente.

Prior to this encounter, the last sighting had been down in the basement. This took place in the ash room, close to the boiler. Will says that his entire team — all six of them — witnessed the shadow man staring at him, before jumping high up into the air, apparently hovering in one of the corners of the ceiling. The figure then changed its shape, going from a human figure to an amorphous black-grey blob, before becoming the face of an old man, complete with jowls and a hangdog expression. It then disappeared, in full view of everybody.

This is a remarkable story, but Will is very certain of what he and his colleagues saw. It seems remarkable that the figure should turn into a caricature of a human face. Usually, shadow figures do not have discernible facial features. This case was different, and things changed again during their encounter up on the third floor. Will claims that he was able to make out the structure of a nose, forehead, and lips. Perhaps most disconcerting of all, he could also see a pair of deep-set, glowing red eyes.

"This wasn't something demonic, or evil," he said. "I think it was more a case of, 'This is *my* space, get the hell out of it.' This thing is ornery and it's mad."

It is interesting to note that 'the Principal' seems to

follow Will as he goes about his business around the school. This apparent attachment to Will may actually help us to determine the shadow figure's identity, as shall be made clear later in this book.

With the benefit of hindsight, he describes the shadow man encounter as, "the coolest thing I've seen in my life!"

Two weeks after the incident, Jonah was back in the school conducting an investigation with two of his team-mates. Standing in almost exactly the same spot on the stairs leading up to the principal's office that Will had been sitting on, he saw what he believed to be a large black mass, lurking in the doorway that led to the auditorium.

Unsure of what to do next, Jonah said something that he still can't quite believe.

"Why don't you run at me as fast as you can?"

Which is exactly what it did.

The dark mass coalesced into a humanoid shape and charged him.

Whereas Will's encounter had been almost completely silent, the shadow man storming toward Jonah was accompanied by a sound that he can only describe as being that of 'something rushing through water.'

His two fellow investigators were also present at the

time. The trio watched in shock as the shadow figure disappeared into thin air, roughly halfway down the length of the corridor, and then reappeared just as suddenly a few feet closer to Jonah. Based upon his description of the encounter, it sounds almost as if the shadow man was phasing in and out of our material plane of reality somehow, which once again lends support to the theory about there being portals on the third floor of the school.

Jonah doesn't recall exactly what happened next, but the sight of the onrushing shadow figure reappearing directly in front of him was enough to make his heart leap into his mouth. The next thing he knew, he was being pushed forcibly backwards, slamming into a cabinet in the principal's office.

He considers himself lucky. If the piece of furniture hadn't broken his momentum, there was a very real chance that Jonah could have been propelled right out of the office window…three stories above the ground.

All in all, he had been pushed backward some eight feet, no mean feat when one considers that Jonah is not particularly small in stature.

I couldn't help but wonder what the third floor would have in store for us over the next few days.

Our next stop was the second floor. We wandered through the classrooms, listening to Will recount just a few of the personal anecdotes that he has gathered during his time at Farrar Elementary. Most of the classrooms still had their chalkboards mounted to the walls, and they were almost entirely covered with the signatures of those who had walked the hallways before us, either because they were visiting out of curiosity, or were like-minded paranormal investigators who wanted to do their part in uncovering some of the mysteries of the old school.

I recognized several of those names, such as John Tenney, Johnny Houser, Chad Lindberg, and Coyote Chris Sutton, to name just a few. There were also plenty of group names listed on those walls. In totality, the number of people who had flocked to Farrar in search of their own brush with the paranormal must have numbered in the high hundreds.

The boys restroom on the second floor was the site of one of the first known EVPs recorded at Farrar, when a visiting psychic named Jacqui captured a little boy's voice saying the words, *She's in the bathroom.* This was said in a somewhat indignant tone of voice, as befitting the mood of a young lad who believed that a girl was using the little boys' room. Based upon the strength of her impressions inside the building that day, the psychic urged owners Jim and Nancy to open the doors of Farrar Elementary to paranormal investigators in order to let them experience it for themselves.

Sadly, Jacqui has since passed away, but all those who have the good fortune to walk inside the front doors of this haunted school owe her a debt of gratitude. Will believes that she is still a presence at the school to this day, and as he mentioned her name, he experienced a sudden chill running through him.

"Yeah, she's still here," he whispered under his breath.

As we strolled along the second floor, I asked Will for his perspective on the haunting. Why, for example, were there so many accounts of child spirits being active in the school, when there were no indications that any children had ever died at Farrar?

As Will explains it, the theory he subscribes to comes largely from his wife, who, like him, believes in a higher power but is not religious in the traditional sense. It is her belief that if somebody lives a good life, then they can essentially create their own form of heaven, whatever that may look like — it would be different for each of us, depending upon our own personal tastes. Essentially, you get to pick your own happy place. For some of the school children, their time at Farrar would have been among the happiest days of their lives. It makes complete sense to us that some of them should choose to return there after their death.

We were in the midst of a discussion about this when I suddenly held up a hand to shush everyone. "Did you guys hear that?" I asked, gesturing toward the far end of the hallway. "I could swear I heard footsteps."

The others nodded. They had heard it too.

"Hello?" Will called, moseying on over in that direction. "Is anybody there?"

Of course, there was nobody to be found. It could have been a screen door, or some other part of the structure settling…or it could have been something else. There was no easy way to tell for sure. Stephen and Erik simply looked at one another and shrugged, as if to say, *Well, that's Farrar for you…*

That was a lesson I was already starting to learn for myself.

"I think there are two negative spirits here," Jonah said, referring to the Principal and the Janitor. "Then there are the children. And there is a protective spirit, who I believe is an adult female."

Interesting...

"About that female entity," Will broke in. "If you come in here politely, you probably won't even know that she's here. But if you come in here acting like a punk, well...you'd better believe she'll let you know she's real. I personally like to think of her as the Librarian."

Although we had no way of knowing it at the time, Will's prediction would turn out to be right on the money — and we would be the recipients of an unbelievably clear piece of direct voice communication that would knock our collective socks off.

So now we had three major spirit players to look out for. The Janitor, the Principal, and the Librarian. Until now, I had been working on the assumption that the Principal was a dark, malevolent entity, but Will wanted to set the record straight where that was concerned.

"He's a good guy, so long as you behave properly. For starters, he likes to be referred to as 'Mr. Principal,'" Will explained. "He likes his title, you see, and he's very protective of this place. Here's an example. Let me tell you about the time I called in a favor from the spirit world..." Will had been in the middle of a spirit box session, getting some excellent interactions from the spirit of a child, when all of a sudden, an older kid's voice broke through. The new speaker unleashed a profanity-laced tirade, dropping F-bombs left, right, and center, supplanting the younger child, who left and never came back. Will was not impressed, to say the least. This wasn't behavior that he was willing to tolerate.

"Mr. Principal," Will had called out to the spirit box.

Yes? came the reply.

Will explained the situation, and asked the Principal if he was willing to take care of things.

Sure.

After a moment of silence from the speaker, the crude youngster disappeared, and the younger child came back.

"That's the Principal in action, you see. He likes to take care of things around here, and you do *not* want him for your enemy…"

Our next stop was the boiler room. To get there, we followed Will down to the gymnasium and hung a left. At the risk of sounding melodramatic, the boiler room definitely did not have a good vibe to it. This might be because it looked like the sort of place where horror movies took place, where monsters lurked in the darkness.

There were lots of dark and shadowy corners, and I kept a watchful eye out for spiders. I didn't know off the top of my head which kinds were native to Iowa, but I was willing to bet that more than a few of them were venomous. I figured it would be just my luck to get a Brown Recluse bite out here in the middle of nowhere. The thought was a chilling one, but as things turned out, spiders were to be the least of my concerns.

As we stood inside the cramped confines of one of what Will called the pump room, listening to him talk about how the boiler room was used for sensory deprivation experiments during some of the public ghost hunts that are run at Farrar, I suddenly caught sight of something moving out of the corner of my eye.

"SNAKE!!!" I let out a high-pitched yelp that would have made Chad Lindberg proud.

The reptile was coiled around the top of one of the water tanks. I'm not going to lie — I damn near jumped out of my skin.

Over the course of my seventeen-year career in the fire and emergency medical services, I have crawled on my hands and knees into burning buildings and patched up my fair share of patients who were spurting blood from horrific injuries. All of that counted for nothing when I caught sight of the snake, which opened its jaws and let out an angry hiss.

I'm a British city boy, born and bred. This was the first wild snake I'd ever seen up close and personal. The fact that I didn't crap my pants was nothing short of remarkable.

For their part, Erik, Stephen, Jonah, and Will were disgustingly unperturbed. "It's just a bull snake," Will shrugged, watching as the creature turned tail and slithered off into the darkness. He chuckled. "Small one, too. Probably about a four-footer. We had an eight-foot son of a bitch in the boiler room one time."

An eight-footer? Screw THAT! I thought. When it came to snakes, I was with Indiana Jones. *Why did it have to be snakes???* Will explained that Bull snakes acted like rattlers when they felt threatened, rearing up and vibrating their tail menacingly in an attempt to make their enemy flee. Though they did bite, there was no envenomation to worry about — it was always a dry bite.

As an aside, I once investigated Fox Hollow Farm in Indiana. Once home to Herb Baumeister, the serial killer known as the I-70 Strangler, the pump room in that particular house was rumored to be the place where he had laid out the bodies of some of his victims, and was also said to be haunted by the ghost of the man himself — something that was borne out when I was caressed on the tricep in there by an unseen hand (for the full story, see *The Horrors of Fox Hollow Farm*, by Richard Estep and Robert Graves). To put things into perspective, one snake was all it took to demote Fox Hollow to being the *second* scariest pump room I had ever investigated...

As if that wasn't fun enough, a rat skittered across one of the pipes that ran high up on the wall. So now we were in a boiler room along with snakes, spiders, *and* rodents.

No thanks.

I couldn't get out of there fast enough. But first, I wanted to hear about the room.

The original boiler was coal driven, and indeed, one can still see the coal chute doors to this day. There is also a room into which the ash was shoveled, and then subsequently extracted via a manhole, though the details of how exactly this was done are unclear.

Will has been instrumental to the success of many of the organized ghost hunts which take place at Farrar Elementary throughout the year. One of his go-to experiments for those events is using the area around the boiler room as a sensory deprivation room, placing hardy souls inside there all alone with their sight and hearing temporarily taken away.

During one such event, an extremely brave fourteen year-old girl had volunteered to be the test subject. A low-light video camera was positioned high up on a sturdy wall-mounted bracket. As the adventurous young lady sat there, all alone in the dark (or free from the company of the living, at least). Will and his companions watch the live feed coming from the camera. To their absolute astonishment, the camera image tilted up and then back down again, as though somebody had grabbed it and pulled it. This happened a total of six times in rapid succession. Will was at a loss for an explanation. Even if the camera mounting hadn't been so high up on the wall that it required climbing a ladder to access it, there was absolutely *nobody* else present in the room, apart from the young lady, who was completely oblivious to the drama that was playing out above her head.

As if that wasn't strange enough, the same thing happened again during the next session. Once again, the camera seemed to temporarily take on a life of its own, nodding up and down several times without apparent cause. When the event was over, Will did his very best to try and debunk what had happened, but close inspection of the camera and its mount revealed that it was solidly placed and could not have been tilted back and forth like that without some kind of direct physical contact.

The only question was what exactly had been manipulating it?

"Personally, I think it was a case of: I showed respect to the spirits, and I got a reward for it," Will mused. We had made our way to the main doors. "Are you guys ready for your three nights at Farrar?"

"I can't wait," I admitted, looking up the staircase toward the second floor.

It was hard to shake the feeling of being watched inside that place, though how much of it was purely psychological was impossible to say.

"Here's my number. Call me if you need me," he said, before adding, "Just don't make me look like an idiot in the book."

Little chance of that. Will is without doubt a smart man who possesses an almost encyclopedic knowledge of the school that he loves so much.

He puts a great deal of thought into the best ways to interact with its resident spirits, and based on the account I had heard from a number of interviewees, I was convinced that he was also something of a lightning rod for the paranormal activity at Farrar.

After we said our goodbyes to Will and Jonah, parting company with warm handshakes all round, Stephen, Erik, and I retired to the break room for a snack and to talk strategy.

By mutual assent, we decided to hit the auditorium first. The entire third floor was the most active, or so the experts told us, and that particular room (along with the principal's office) was where much of the bizarre phenomena was said to take place.

The sunlight was beginning to fade by the time we went up there. The atmosphere at Farrar was already beginning to feel subtly different, though it was difficult to explain exactly how. I walked to one of the auditorium windows and looked outside. The shadows of the trees outside were getting long, stretching across the ground, while above us, the first stars were coming out.

Stephen and Erik immediately set to work, placing equipment at strategic intervals all around the auditorium. After starting my digital voice recorder running, I set it down gently on the edge of the stage and climbed the wooden steps to take a seat in the comfortable old armchair.

Will had explicitly warned us not to sit in that chair late at night, as it was so comfortable, we would almost immediately fall asleep. Now, as I sank down into the soft cushions with a contented little grunt, I had to admit that he was right. This was a *damn* comfortable chair.

Squatting in one of the corners, Stephen was placing an EMF sensor, while Erik was getting his own audio recorder up and running.

Thud.

We all froze. It had come from somewhere behind me, in the shadowy recesses of the stage.

"That sounded like a footstep," Erik said, stating the obvious.

He was right. It really had.

I fumbled in my hip pocket for a flashlight, shining the beam into the darkness. Everything was still and quiet.

"Come on out," Stephen called cheerfully, reaching into his bag for another sensor. "We've brought some toys for you to play with…"

Thud. Thud.

Two more steps, one after the other in rapid succession, came once again from the back of the stage. We looked at one another, eyebrows raised, and then set out to debunk the sound. It hadn't been a water pipe or a piece of equipment. No sound like it had been heard inside the school all day. This hadn't sounded mechanical anyway, nor had it been the noise made by a rodent or some other critter; it was exactly like the sound that the sole of a shoe makes when it strikes the floor.

"This is your show," Stephen said, emphasizing to the spirits of Farrar that they had our total respect. He switched on a series of EM pumps, devices that were designed to flood the room with electromagnetic energy in the hope that spirit entities would be able to use it as fuel, or to manipulate it somehow.

We sat there quietly, waiting patiently as dusk turned to full darkness. There was very little ambient light coming through the windows, and none whatsoever from the hallway outside the auditorium.

This was a habit that many paranormal investigators were fond of adopting in a supposedly haunted location — simply sitting there, in the very best of company, slowly acclimatizing to the structure, and letting the building itself grow accustomed to us.

Erik began to experience some strange visual disturbances, finding it difficult to make out any details in the near-total darkness. He was the first to admit that this may simply have been down to "my middle-aged eyes," but we found it interesting that this was also accompanied by a sense of the chills running through his body.

Was the old school beginning to wake up for the evening?

We waited. It got darker. There were no further unexplained noises. The three of us chatted in hushed tones, while also keeping our eyes and ears peeled for anything out of the ordinary.

Every once in a while, a flash of bright white light would dance across the wall to our left. Our initial excitement gave way to disappointment after a little further investigation revealed the cause: every time a car crested the top of a nearby hill, its headlights would splash across the auditorium for just a fraction of a second. This was a relatively quick and easy debunk, particularly when we began to pay closer attention to the distant sound of car engines right before the lights appeared.

Not all mysteries at Farrar would be so easily solved.

Time passed slowly, with little in the way of results to show for it. In that regard, it was like any of a hundred other paranormal investigations we had been involved with. As the psychically sensitive ones, Stephen and Erik would almost certainly pick up on anything of significance long before I did.

Gradually, things began to lighten. The moon was rising, and had moved round to shine through the back windows. Our eyes slowly adjusted to the low-light conditions. Erik quietly asked the spirits if they would be kind enough to move an object, or give some other sign of their presence.

"I don't want you to feel like circus monkeys, jumping through hoops or anything," he said, before adding, "I know that you get people coming through here practically every day, asking for that."

Stephen began to ask some of the standard EVP questions, firing off a quick thirty-second burst and then playing it back. There was nothing on the recording other than the sound of his own voice.

A little disappointed, we decided to change positions. Coming down from the stage, we spread out into the center of the auditorium.

Roughly twenty minutes later, we each began to see tiny red points of light flashing across the wall behind us. Erik went to stand by the window, and verified that this time, the lights were not those of a passing car. All three of us saw them, each at different times. The lights were only there for a split-second, and defied our attempts to photograph them.

Whereas I saw red lights, Stephen would see both red *and* yellow lights. I couldn't help but wonder whether his psychic sensitivity was allowing him a slightly broader window into the light phenomena than my plain vanilla brain had. Erik saw neither on this particular occasion, but had witnessed the same red lights that I saw on a prior visit.

Erik told me that every time he and his colleagues from AAPI had visited Farrar Elementary for an investigation, they had *all* seen similar LED-sized points of multicolored light in the auditorium. Nobody had been able to debunk the sightings yet. The lights had appeared all around the room, including the back of the stage. We spent some time trying to find an explanation, ranging from a smoke alarm/carbon monoxide sensor (didn't explain the multiple colors) and outside light sources (no light was shining through the windows when we saw the lights) to reflections from the spectacles of the observer (I wasn't wearing any).

What I was beginning to think of as the phantom lights were an intriguing unknown, just one of many that we would encounter inside the old schoolhouse.

The AAPI folks had also seen a lot of moving shadows out in the third-floor hallway, and I tried to keep the doorways leading out there in my line of sight at all times.

Nothing seemed to be rising up to take the bait. Despite the light anomalies that Stephen and I had seen, the atmosphere felt decidedly flat. The rather odd feeling of being watched that I had felt on first entering the school had gone.

Perhaps the three of us were alone in there.

"This isn't working," I said after a while, trying not to let my frustration show. We had been at it for hours, and although the unexplained sounds and lights had made for a promising start, it was beginning to feel as if things were fizzling out.

Stephen suggested that we take a break, which sounded like a good idea to Erik and I. We made our way downstairs for some snacks. Sinking back into the comfortable couch, I stifled a massive yawn, then cracked open an energy drink and took a long swallow. It was early in the morning now, and all three of us were starting to get tired.

After a bit of discussion, we agreed that our energy levels were low, in every sense of the word. In other words, not only were we weary and moving sluggishly, our mental and emotional energy levels were flagging too. Small wonder that nothing of a paranormal nature was manifesting. We weren't exactly giving it the psychic energy equivalent of a free buffet lunch.

"We either need to get our energy levels up, or call it a night," Stephen said, telling it like it was.

"I don't want to turn in this early," Erik replied. "But how do you propose we get our energy levels up?"

My answer was drinking enough caffeine to float a small battleship, but Stephen had a more radical idea. "Let's hit the gym."

"What?" Erik raised an eyebrow. "You do realize that we're three middle-aged, out-of-shape guys, right?'

Stephen waved his half-kidding objection away with a dismissive hand. "I'm totally serious. The school is supposed to be haunted by the spirits of kids, right? Well, what's stopping us from going down there and kicking a ball around?"

Evidently nothing, because ten minutes later we were doing just that. There were several plastic balls of varying sizes in the gymnasium. Leaving the lights down at their lowest setting, we began to kick a soccer ball back and forth. Before I knew it, I was having the time of my life, running from one end of the game court to the other, trying to resurrect the pitifully bad soccer skills I had developed as a young lad.

Erik and Stephen were no slouches either, and before long we had a pretty good kick about going on. It wasn't long before all three of us managed to break a sweat. Erik fired off a particularly wicked right cross that flew past my left leg, hit the far wall behind me, bounced, and then disappeared…into the pitch blackness of the boiler room.

I looked back over my shoulder at the entrance to the boiler room. All I could think of was what we had found in there on Will's tour.

"Don't look at me, lads," I said. "You couldn't pay me a thousand dollars to go in there again. Who knows where that bloody snake has gotten to!"

"Good point." Erik jogged over to the far corner of the room and came back with a cheap basketball.

"Now you're talking!" Stephen grinned. "Come on, let's shoot some hoops."

Which is exactly what we did. We took it in turns to stand a few meters in front of the hoop and, bouncing on our toes, lob the ball in a semi-graceful arc toward the net. Most bounced off the rim of the net or the back wall itself, but what we lacked in skill and coordination, the three of us more than made up for with tenacity and raw enthusiasm.

Normally, I wouldn't have had a prayer at hitting the net a single time, but unbeknownst to Steven and Erik, I had a secret weapon. My ambulance had been posted at Fire Station One in Longmont a few weeks before, and the firefighters had roped me into their now-traditional basketball game workout. With a lot of coaching, this clueless English boy had learned to hit the net maybe one time in three, usually bouncing the ball off the back of it first.

It also didn't hurt that tonight I was up against a pair of equally ungainly and uncoordinated middle-aged guys. Erik and I were more than a little embarrassed that a grey-haired Catholic priest wearing spandex leggings was running rings around the pair of us. Stephen, for his part, was cheerfully unrepentant about showing us both up.

But the key point was that we were laughing, joking, and having a good time. Each time the ball arced through the air and slammed into the net, we gave a raucous cheer. When it bounced off and flew away into the darkness, we groaned. It was a deliberate attempt to recapture some of the happy energy that must have been generated in that very same gym over the decades, when countless games of basketball, soccer, and other team sports were played by generation after generation. We were hoping to connect with some of the spirit energies of the past by doing the exact same thing that they had done, in the same place.

By the end of the game, all three of us were huffing and puffing like steam trains going uphill. Then we launched straight into an EVP session.

"Is anybody here?" Stephen called out. "Does anybody want to say hi, or come and play with us?"

No answer came out of the darkness, but in the doorway to the boiler room, a large shadow moved, darting off to the left. Erik swung his flashlight beam around to follow it, but it had disappeared into the greater blackness at the periphery of the gymnasium.

I was hoping that one of the many brightly-colored balls would come rolling out of the darkness toward us, but that would have been too perfect... too Hollywood. This was real life, and for now at least, nothing was moving inside the gymnasium but the three of us — and whatever the shadow had been. It was impossible to tell if it had truly been a shadow *figure* or not, because of the sheer speed with which it moved. In fact, it was impossible to discount it entirely as having been a simple trick of the light. Farrar was notorious for its shadow figure activity, but that didn't mean that the eyes (or the mind) weren't capable of playing tricks on us.

"Do you mind that we're playing games in here?" Stephen continued, panning the beam of his flashlight slowly around the gym. He was, I knew, looking for shadow figures that might be standing totally still and watching us.

Stephen stopped his own voice recorder and played back the audio from the past few minutes. I left mine running, recording the playback. Although we didn't understand why, this particular technique — recording the recording — sometimes yielded some incredible EVPs, but only on the *second* recording.

Some would say that noise artifact had been introduced during this process (in much the same way that an image gets increasingly distorted the more times you photocopy it) but we had, in the past, heard the most remarkably clear voices speaking in this manner.

Not this time, however. The voices were silent. If there truly *had* been somebody watching us in the gymnasium, then they were keeping to themselves.

Once again, we had struck out.

What was it with this place? I wondered, shaking my

head. Things had started off strong, but despite our very best efforts to drum up some activity, not a damned thing of note had happened apart from the footsteps up on the third floor and the brief glimpse of a moving shadow downstairs in the gym.

Had all the stories I'd heard about this place been just that — stories? Were Stephen and Erik, Will and Jonah, not to mention John Tenney and Chad Lindberg, all wrong about the school?

I had no way of knowing that, in just a few minutes' time, that question would be answered in the most unequivocal way.

We were well into the early hours of the morning. So far that night, Farrar Elementary had given us a few on-demand noises and light phenomena, along with a moving shadow that may or may not have been paranormal. Stephen and Erik were a little more impressed with some of them than I was. I thought it likely that their prior experiences at Farrar had maybe biased them a little in favor of the place being haunted.

I had no idea that a knockout punch was waiting for me, lurking right around the corner.

After chilling out and shooting the breeze in the break

room for a few minutes, we got off the much-too-comfortable couches, and stepped into the hallway directly outside the break room. The staircase was directly off to our left.

As the three of us stood quietly at the foot of the staircase, we suddenly heard the unmistakable sound of footsteps, walking around somewhere above us on the third floor. We all looked at one another, as if to say, *Do you hear that?* It was plain to see that we all did.

I'm not entirely sure what came over me, but I just couldn't help it. Cheerfully, I craned my head upward and hollered, *"Heeeeellooooo!!!"*

Everything went quiet. The footsteps stopped. Several seconds passed, and then—

"HELLO."

"Shit — did you hear *that?!?*" My head snapped up. We had all heard it. A woman's voice, soft, lilting, but as clear as a bell, repeating my greeting back to me. The timbre had an ethereal quality to it that is hard to describe, but sounded almost as if the woman had been calling out to us from the far end of a tunnel. It had originated somewhere upstairs, from the darkness of the upper floor.

It had been a direct voice. Not an EVP, something

recorded after the fact, but rather an intelligent response. Such things are extremely rare in the field of paranormal field research. I had heard of maybe a handful of instances happening to people I knew, but in almost 25 years of investigating, had never experienced it myself.

Until now.

The three of us looked at one another in what I can only assume must have been a Three Stooges-like way.

"That was either a young boy, or a woman," declared Stephen.

"Sounded like a woman to me," Erik said.

I suddenly experienced a flash of self-doubt. The voice had been SO clear that I actually started to wonder if it had been real.

"That couldn't have been my echo, could it?"

Both of my friends shook their heads. It was actually a pretty ridiculous thing for me to think, if only because of the fact that the response had taken at least five seconds to be spoken. There were no acoustics anywhere in Farrar that would delay sound waves for five whole seconds.

"That was a disembodied voice, I promise you...and it was amazing," said Erik. He was right — it was.

"Let's get up there." Stephen was already climbing the

stairs, taking them two at a time. Erik and I were right on his heels. A loud thud came from somewhere up above us on the third floor. We made it up there in no time at all, and began searching all of the rooms methodically, one by one.

Of course, they were all empty.

The building was locked up tight. Although it was possible that somebody could have broken in without us seeing or hearing them, it should be pointed out that there were no signs of breaking and entering. Every door and window was still secured, just as they had been at the start of the evening. Besides, was somebody *really* going to break into an old school in the middle of rural Iowa at 2am, creep upstairs, and then wait in the hopes that somebody would call out, so that they could try and spook them? The very idea of it was preposterous.

Although the owners, Jim and Nancy, do live on-site, they had not left their residence that evening. We confirmed this the following day. Nancy was recovering from an illness, and wasn't remotely up to climbing several flights of stairs and hiding in a dark and dusty classroom. We also feel very comfortable in saying that with his gruff voice, Jim really wouldn't make much of a female impersonator...and the voice that all three of us heard was definitely that of a woman.

In my view, at least, there was no question about it — we had just experienced the paranormal phenomenon known as 'direct voice.' That alone made it worth driving all the way from Colorado to Iowa for.

And then it dawned on us — we didn't have an audio recorder running. Talk about making a rookie mistake. We'd been recording continuously for most of the night up 'til then. Unfortunately, once we set foot inside the break room, all three of us had adopted the mindset that we were, well, *on a break*... and had kicked back to relax a little. That had also, regrettably, included switching off our equipment.

With hindsight, the stupidity of our thinking was obvious, and we should have known better. A haunted location doesn't take breaks. Just because we declared it to be down-time, didn't mean that whatever was active at Farrar would do the same. Why would it?

Lesson learned. From that point on, we ran our recorders constantly.

I did cut myself a little bit of slack though. The next day, while we had gathered in the break room again, we re-watched the episode of *Ghost Stalkers* on my tablet. Erik pointed out that when he took his turn to investigate, John

Tenney had experienced what at first seemed like a bizarre malfunction with his voice recorder: when he was using it to record himself talking while inside the elementary school, the sound of his own voice was somehow removed from the playback. Yet when he stepped outside, the recorder operated as normal, recording his words clearly. Going back inside the school once more, the recorder again refused to play ball.

It was almost as if the entities inside Farrar didn't want evidence of their existence to be captured. After all, eyewitness accounts and anecdotal evidence are one thing — but recordings that could be played back and analyzed ad infinitum are something else entirely. Did that mean that if we *had* been recording continuously, the mysterious woman's voice would not have spoken to us? It's entirely possible, and frankly made a great Band-Aid to slap on our own embarrassment at missing such an incredible opportunity to record a great piece of evidence.

After 'clearing' the third floor of potential human intruders, we decided to make our way to Mrs. Martin's classroom and sit there for a while. Each of us took a seat and settled down to relax in the darkness. We sat there for a while, talking quietly amongst ourselves. I was desperately hoping the unknown female would pipe up again.

"Can you please make a noise out in the hallway again?" Erik asked. Precisely on cue, he got an answer: a very solid bang came from outside in the hallway, just as he had requested. He was every bit as pleased with this unexpected result as Stephen and I were. "Thank you!"

Next, he asked the spirit communicator if they would be willing and capable of closing the classroom door. There was no immediate response, but then a few seconds later, two more thumps came from outside in the deserted hallway.

We were all in agreement that the spirits of Farrar had already more than made good on their reputation that night.

They weren't quite done with us yet, however.

Stephen asked if they would please make another noise, just to confirm that they really were present. No sooner were the words out of his mouth than we all heard the distinct sound of a thud coming from outside the classroom.

"Damn," I said, impressed. We were getting physical responses to our questions, and they were coming entirely on cue.

"Thanks for doing that," Stephen called out. "We really appreciate it." And he was right — we really *did* appreciate the interaction that we were getting. Most haunted locations weren't *nearly* as active as Farrar Elementary was turning out to be.

Things quietened down significantly after that. The hallway noises stopped happening almost as abruptly as they had started. We sat there for twenty more minutes, just to make absolutely sure, but ultimately came to the conclusion that things were winding down for the night — totally understandable, as the sky outside the windows was beginning to lighten. Daybreak was just around the corner, and it was getting to be that time of the morning when even the most active location usually starts to drain of energy and return to a dormant state.

At the end of the night, as we said goodbye to the spirits (they never answered) and locked the main entrance doors behind us, I was completely satisfied that Farrar Elementary was haunted. That voice had been too clear, too *real*, to allow me to come to any other conclusion.

Who was the woman? The answer to *that* particular question wouldn't come for several months, when I interviewed a number of expert witnesses about the case. For now, I sat in the passenger seat of our car. As Erik drove slowly down the long driveway, I couldn't take my eyes off the school in the rearview mirror. I half-expected to see the figure of a woman looking back at us from one of the third-floor windows, illuminated by the brilliant white moonlight.

Erik turned onto the road and soon, the school was out of sight. We were all tired, but exuberant, the direct voice allowing us to go out on a high note. I could hardly wait to see what the school would have in store for us tomorrow.

Day 2 - E. E. Bensen

Sunday, September 23, 2018.

Given that the Farrar School was only a little over two hours away, we opted to stop by another of our favorite Iowa haunts, Malvern Manor. There were day tours in progress, and we were greeted by fellow paranormal investigators Chris Case and Luis Taz Cruz. We had a fun conversation about all things paranormal, and also about some shocking recent discoveries regarding the manor (which will be shared publicly in due course, but it is not my place to do so). After taking a brief stroll through the building, we decided to continue our journey to Farrar. (Check out Richard's book,

The Devil's Coming to Get Me, for a history of Malvern Manor, as well as a blow-by-blow account of our investigation of the place in October of 2017).

We arrived in the Iowa town of Ankeny a few hours later, checked in to our hotel, and grabbed a heavy dinner at a nearby steakhouse. Little did we know that a couple days of out of the ordinary food during the road trip, combined with that meal, would lead to what can only be described as a gastrointestinal tour de force later that night. I won't go into graphic detail, but it was pretty hilarious. Audio evidence may or may not exist.

Meandering through the farm fields, rolling hills, and perfectly manicured green lawns of the accompanying homes, we eventually arrived at the Farrar schoolhouse. I'm always struck by just how pretty that area of Iowa really is.

The school itself is a bit of an anomaly as it is just not the type of building that you would expect to see in such a rural, small town area. It is three stories high and has a brown brick exterior. There are a couple of houses nearby, along with a church and a cemetery across the street.

I turned into the long gravel driveway and parked the SUV adjacent to the front door.

We found owner Jim Oliver, caretaker Will Conkel, and

paranormal investigator Jonah Jones waiting for us on the front step.

Jim greeted us cheerfully as usual, and we spent a few minutes engaged in small talk. Regrettably, during this time it became apparent that this part of Iowa was in the middle of some sort of mosquito plague apocalypse. It was somewhat amusing to watch I'm sure, as Richard, Stephen, and I kept swiping randomly in the air, on our bodies, and rubbing our exposed arms.

Will and Jonah proceeded to give us a tour of the property. While Stephen and I had been there multiple times in the past, it was Richard's first visit, and given the book project at hand it just made sense to do.

We started by walking the outside property where Will gave us a lay of the land, as well as pointed out Native American activity in the area in times past.

It is not often that Richard and I feel height challenged, as we are both in the six-foot-two to six-foot-four range, however Will towered over us by about four inches.

It is safe to say that the three of us together would produce one of the least desirable targets for a mugging as is possible.

Will struck me as a very outspoken, honest, tough, no

BS kind of guy. Some folks just have a good energy about them that you know you can identify with, and I liked him immediately. Jonah is intensely interested in paranormal research and was eager to share his experiences with us as well. A relative newcomer to the field, the three of us agreed later that his enthusiasm is something that we had all shared years ago before becoming as jaded as we are today. It is certainly infectious, and he is definitely a kindred spirit as well. I suspect we'll see a lot more of him in the field in the years to come.

It quickly became clear that the mosquitoes were far more interested in us than they were of the Iowa boys, so I guess Colorado blood was a delicacy on the menu that night. I am not sure how many bites I received in the 20 to 30 minutes we were out there, but it was a lot. I continued to spend the entirety of that time outdoors rubbing my arms and swatting at random intervals like a psychopath. Eventually we entered the building and proceeded to visit each area systematically. Will and Jonah relayed various experiences they'd had in the building as we made our way through its halls. Of particular interest to me, were the reports of the shadow man, or, the Principal, as some call it. A sighting of this particular entity is very common in the building, and I wanted to hear about as many of them as I could in light of my own experience.

We entered the lower floor boiler room, which is generally regarded as a hot spot in the building for paranormal activity. It is exactly what you would probably imagine, and looks like it could be used as a shooting location for a *Nightmare on Elm Street* movie. Upon entering a small pump room off to the left, a fairly large bull snake coiled on top of a storage tank began to slither away from us. Richard nearly had a heart attack which was very amusing to watch, as Will gently nudged it with his finger saying, "Aww, it's just a bull snake, he won't hurt ya."

We didn't bother to investigate that particular room. Will relayed a story of coming face to face with the shadow man in the boiler room, reporting that he was close enough to actually see facial features such as the outline of eyes, cheeks, and a nose. I found this extremely impressive as it is rare to experience such detail.

As we continued our tour, eventually we reached the top floor which is generally considered to be the most active from a paranormal perspective. I certainly cannot argue with that assertion as it is where the auditorium is located, and where I had my own personal encounter with the shadow man nearly three years prior. Jonah recounted a story where he had been standing at one end of the hallway on the few stairs leading up into a small office overlooking the floor known as the principal's office, and had witnessed this shadow figure appear at the opposite end of the hallway. He indicated to us that he had called out and asked nicely if it could get a little bit closer to him.

In what is most certainly an exercise in being careful of what one should wish for, in the blink of an eye, the shadow figure covered the length of the hallway and reached Jonah, where he reported being pushed backwards, and ended up falling down onto a filing cabinet in the principal's office. With a playful smile, Will was quick to point out that the cabinet still won't close properly as a result. This event really should serve as a lesson for any aspiring paranormal investigator to be cautious in what she or he asks for.

Interestingly, Jonah feels a very negative intent from this figure, and of the haunting of the school as a whole. I don't share this viewpoint based on my own experiences, but that certainly doesn't make it invalid. It is quite possible that any sort of haunting experience had by any given individual would have somewhat of a personal slant to it. I've not felt threatened by anything in the school to date, however I certainly do tend to feel on edge in there at night. So far, I have assumed that this is due to the fact I personally have proof that the place is unequivocally haunted. It would be difficult for most people to wander around a place like Farrar alone in the dark, while knowing that they were not the "only" presence in there, and not end up feeling at least somewhat anxious. I also found it particularly interesting that Will seemed to have no fear of the place whatsoever. He has certainly spent more time in there than most people, and I'm sure that does help, but in my opinion, he was almost shockingly at ease. I figure that either Will simply has a bigger set of balls than the rest of us, or there is some other underlying reason yet to be uncovered. I view both options as real possibilities, but I prefer the latter and don't need to know details regarding the former.

At the conclusion of the tour, Will and Jonah headed home thus leaving the three of us to explore the schoolhouse on our own. That evening we put our gear into the small office area on the first floor that is set aside as a break room, or 'home base,' for visiting investigators. Grabbing some basic equipment such as digital recorders and flashlights, we set out to wander the hallways and classrooms systematically, until eventually making our way to the top floor auditorium where we proceeded to hang out for quite some time. Richard took a comfortable chair that was placed on the stage, Stephen took one down on the main floor area along the wall, and I opted to sit on the edge of the stage itself.

It was extremely dark in the room, to the point that I could not make out my hand in front of my face. There was only a small amount of light coming in from the window at the far back of the room, and it took quite a while for my eyes to adjust. Still, walking around without a flashlight would have been very hazardous. At best I could only make out the general shape of the room in the inky blackness. I am sure that having spent significant time in there during past visits greatly aided in what little capacity I had to orient myself.

After taking a seat on the edge of the stage, almost immediately I heard what can only be described as movement and perhaps light footsteps behind me at the rear of the stage.

Richard called it out as well, and for a few minutes we listened to these sounds on and off. At one point I got up and explored the area with my flashlight upon Richard's suggestion that perhaps it was an animal. I found nothing of the sort or any droppings to suggest that one had been in the area. Is it possible that an animal was inside of the wall or under the stage perhaps?

Of course it is. There is no way to call this particular experience "paranormal", so I'll have to leave it for what it is, an anomaly worthy of mentioning but nothing more.

We certainly heard something, but I just don't know what it was. I will point out that we spent a significant amount of time in that room during our three days in the building, and never heard it again, for whatever that is worth.

A few minutes later as we were sitting in silence and I was again marveling at just how dark it was in the room, I began to notice what can only be described as billowing gray visual phenomena filling the space. It almost looked like smoke, which is the best description that I can come up with for it. Naturally I assumed it was my eyes, and I sat there for several minutes just taking it in and not saying anything about it.

Eventually it occurred to me that shortly before, my eyes had indeed adjusted to the darkness, and I was able to make out some things very faintly in the room with no problem. Now, I couldn't see a thing. Granted, at 44 I am starting to get somewhat older, and my eyesight is gradually fading as everyone's inevitably will, however this was something out of the ordinary. I've never had my eyes adjust *twice* in a dark area.

After pondering for a little while longer, and not convinced that it was anything worth mentioning, I sheepishly reported what I was seeing to the others in the interest of doing a thorough paranormal investigation. To my utter surprise, Stephen quickly said that he was having the same exact experience. I asked if it had started several minutes prior and out of the blue, and he confirmed that it had. Richard indicated that he wasn't noticing anything out of the norm.

A few minutes later, whatever I was seeing was gone, and again Stephen reported that he was able to see normally at the same time. I don't think either one of us was convinced at that moment that what we were seeing was paranormal in any way, but still, the coincidence of both of us having the same experience at the same time was interesting. We have investigated with each other for countless hours now, and that had never happened before. It was not until two days later that Will and his wife Jacquelyn would join us for a few hours of investigation in this very room, and describe to us phenomena that were surprisingly similar to what Stephen and I were experiencing. Perhaps there was more going on than we were giving it credit for at the time.

We continued to sit in the auditorium for quite some time, and eventually as I was staring at the floor in the middle of the room, I caught a glimpse of a small point of yellow light zip across from right to left and vanish just as quickly. Neither of the others saw this, unfortunately, however a few minutes later Stephen reported seeing the same thing in another part of the room. Shortly after that, Richard reported seeing a red one. These strange moving pinpoints of light are something that I have witnessed numerous times during investigations, and most notably for our purposes here, in this very room at Farrar on all past visits. In many cases, these have been seen by multiple investigators simultaneously, thus removing any skeptical speculation that it could be misfiring receptors in the eye or some other purely optic nerve related visual anomaly.

A few years ago, during an investigation of the Old Tooele Hospital, the five of us present all saw the same moving points of light several times over the course of a half hour. I have no idea what they are, but I can assure the reader that it is a real manifestation of "something". Is it paranormal? I have no idea. I saw numerous instances of these same phenomena over the course of this investigation, in a variety of colors.

Eventually we made our way back to home base on the first floor, and spent a few minutes relaxing and having snacks while fiddling around with our phones. Suddenly, I heard a muffled voice in the room directly above us which would be a second-floor classroom. It was indistinct, but definitely either female or that of a child. At least one of the others heard it as well, and over the course of the next few minutes it happened a few more times. Then we began to hear strange taps and shuffling noises also coming from the second floor. The office we were in is situated right next to the stairway, and the school is a very effective echo chamber. When it is quiet in there, you can hear just about anything coming from any floor, at least somewhat.

The noises continued several times. They were brief, but very pronounced, and I was intrigued given how quickly we started hearing them after the voices. At one point, we heard another shuffle and a tap or click, and I called out loudly, "Hey if that was you up there, can you do it again please?" Without hesitation, the exact same sound happened again on command.

While it is true that we are all aging, and somewhat lazy as a result, the instantly repeated noise (which seemed to directly respond to us) was enough to make us grab our gear again, and walk back out into the hallway. The fact that the voices wouldn't keep talking is perhaps somewhat embarrassing, but I've already established that we are pretty jaded; at least, that is my excuse, and I'm sticking to it. We stood for a few moments at the foot of the stairs in absolute silence before hearing yet another shuffling sound from the second floor. Richard was in front of Stephen and me, and looked inquisitively up at the high ceiling of the stairwell in the direction of the second floor. He then loudly said, "Hello?" We were rewarded seconds later with a very clear female disembodied voice emanating from the top of the stairs that repeated a friendly sounding, "Hello!"

I raised an eyebrow, smiled slyly, and looked at Stephen who was already eyeing me with a satisfied and unsurprised smirk. Richard snapped his head around and looked directly at me. I think the expression on his face would have been roughly the same if I had somehow slipped on a big fluffy Easter bunny mask without him knowing and had surprised him with my visage. He was clearly shocked, and I got quite a bit of amusement out of this. After a very quick and noble attempt to debunk it as an echo of his own voice, Stephen and I reassured him that it was indeed female, had different inflection (enthusiastic versus inquisitive), and in *no way* could have been an echo. Later he indicated to us that after 25 or so years of trying to get that to happen, this was the first time he'd ever actually gotten such a direct reply. His reaction made more sense to me at that point. AAPI has been extremely fortunate in this area, as we have had many instances of direct and audible voice responses to us. I know that it is not common in general, and I am immensely thankful for our many experiences like this. It never ceases to be one of the coolest possible things that can happen during a paranormal investigation: speaking directly to "thin air" and having a reply emanate from seemingly nothing.

We quickly proceeded up the stairs to the second floor to make sure that nobody else was there. Naturally, and not unexpectedly, there was no one to be found. We had the place locked down after all. The nature of the echoes in the building would have prevented anyone from making an undetected escape as well. On top of that, the voice had the usual disembodied distortion to it. It was clear, but it was also definitely not physical as in emanating from a voice box like a human voice does. These almost sound as though they are coming through a small speaker, but tend to be 'fuller' in overall quality, if that makes any sense.

After a few minutes we took a seat in the second-floor classroom at the top of the primary staircase in front of the main entrance. Again, strange clicks, bangs, and shuffling noises were heard in the hallway just outside at odd intervals of perhaps three to five minutes. Also, once again, I asked for a repeat performance, and was rewarded with the same sound on command. Eventually the noises subsided and we continued roaming the school when all went quiet again.

Next, we entered the gymnasium on the basement level and hung out in there for quite some time. There were a few somewhat deflated toy balls lying around, so we proceeded to give a master class in how *not* to shoot hoops.

Seriously, the miss rate really was both stunning and embarrassing in equal measure. Growing bored of our shattered NBA dreams, we wandered around the gym floor for a while calling out hopefully for replies or any other sign of paranormal activity. As I casually swept my large flashlight beam past the door to the boiler room in the corner of the gym, Stephen had already been looking that way and reported catching a glimpse of an extremely tall shadow figure standing just inside the doorway that perfectly sidestepped the light as it began to illuminate the door frame and eventually the room beyond.

This came as little surprise to me as I know that a shadow man, or whatever it may be, is in that school. The area that it stepped into is not wide open, proving once again that physical boundaries mean nothing to whatever it is. That is both interesting, and maybe on some deep- down level, a little scary too.

We wrapped the first night of investigation in the wee hours of the morning and made our way back to the hotel for some rest. On the roughly half hour drive, we compared notes and experiences, and concluded that even if absolutely nothing else happened in the next two days, we would not leave disappointed. A direct disembodied voice response and a shadow figure are two pretty huge experiences.

If that was all that Farrar would give to us during this investigation, we would head back to Denver quite content. Luckily, the infamous shadow man was not quite done showing himself to us yet. he remote schoolhouse still had a few strange experiences to share with us...

Chapter Three

Day 3 – Richard Estep

Before going back inside the school the next day, Stephen, Erik, and I had discussed our strategy well in advance (one of the benefits of a long car journey). We were all in complete agreement.

Although each of us had enough equipment to outfit a small engineering workshop, we were only going to use it sparingly.

We have been investigating claims of the paranormal for many years, and had all started out being very tech-heavy; I for one remember running hundreds of meters of cables to remote cameras and microphones, sometimes spending a quarter of my on-scene time on equipment setup.

Then you had to tear it all down again at the end of the night. After that came the real killer: evidence review, the bane of almost every paranormal investigator's existence.

Hour upon hour of mindless tedium, watching video playback on monitor screens until your eyes feel like they're going to bleed. Listening to what seems like an endless stream of audio files, conversations that you've already listened to before being played back again, and straining your ears to make out the faintest whisper of an EVP.

My philosophy now is that at 45 years of age, I am too old for all of that. While it had yielded a scattering of good results, the dividends weren't remotely worth the outlay in terms of my valuable time and overall happiness (all those hours of evidence review tend to make you a little bit cranky, as my wife will attest).

Ever since I'd begun writing books set in the paranormal non-fiction genre, I had begun approaching my cases from less of a technical standpoint and more of a narrative one.

I liked taking readers along with me on my ghost adventures, using prose to place them in a pitch-black hallway in a place like Farrar, trying to convey the mood and the emotions that my colleagues and I were feeling. I wanted my readers to get a sense of what it was like to be in the middle of a haunted building, alone in the dark and feeling all too vulnerable, rather than sitting in front of a laptop and staring at the screen.

So, the upshot was that Stephen, Erik, and I had resolved to drastically curtail our use of technology, substituting good old human experience instead, with all the bias and subjectivity that came along with it. We would attempt to stimulate and engage with the spirits of Farrar Elementary as best we could, and see if they were willing to come out and play.

To that end, when we arrived back at the school late the following afternoon, we went back downstairs into the gymnasium. Although long past its prime, the biggest room in the school was the center of attention on more than one occasion in the past.

It is said that none other than the renowned Harlem Globetrotters played basketball there at one point. In addition to its use as a sporting arena, the gym was also the scene of dances and other social events, including one funeral — that of a local psychic who felt particularly drawn to Farrar, and the ghostly children that she insisted still haunted the place and wanted their stories to be told.

Will had told us that the gym was the scene of a paranormal audio phenomenon in which the sounds of sporting games long since finished could still be heard today — the sounds of shoes pounding on the floor, the cheers and roars of the crowd, and the applause that arose whenever a player scored. While almost certainly a residual phenomenon (a form of paranormal recording) we found this to be intriguing.

The three of us walked into the gym. How best to drum up a little energy? The answer seemed obvious, just as it had the night before. The array of colorful balls of all shapes and sizes were still scattered all around the place, sitting exactly where we'd left them.

Scooping them up, we began hurling them toward the closest basketball net, trying to get a slam dunk with balls that were much smaller and lighter than basketballs. I'm ashamed to say that it took me fifteen attempts to get one into the net for the first time. So much for having gotten in a little practice.

Erik fared better this time, sinking two or three for every one of mine. With the lights out in the gym, we were playing by the faint glow coming from the light at the bottom of the stairs.

When we switched to kicking the ball instead of throwing it, things got a little more interesting. You would hear the ball being kicked at the opposite end of the gym, try to follow the sound of it skittering across the floor, and then suddenly it would appear flying out of the darkness right at you.This forced you. to react quickly in order to send it back towards your opponent.

In our minds, we were picturing it as being something like the infamous volleyball scene from the movie *Top Gun* — minus the shirtless aspect, thank goodness. In reality, we were three middle-aged men who got out of breath climbing a few flights of stairs. It wasn't long before the gasping and moaning noises we made were interspersed with loud farts and belches, which reduced us all to giggling juveniles. It's funny how quickly grown men can regress to the mental state of five-year-old boys under certain circumstances.

At this point, you might be thinking, "Really? Am I supposed to take these guys serious as paranormal investigators? They sound like a bunch of kids." But that was the whole point. If the school was haunted primarily by the spirits of children, as the conventional wisdom stated, then what better way to engage with them than by coming down to their level? This was *exactly* how I had behaved in the school gym when I was a kid, back when the bray of a loud fart seemed like the very epitome of sophisticated humor. Would phantom children be likely to respond to the dry, utterly serious method traditionally employed by some investigators ("Is there anybody there? Tell us your name...") or would they be more likely to respond to playground behavior like this? My money was on the latter.

There was also the possibility of annoying the principal. Although we operated from a position of respect where the spirits of any given location were concerned, we weren't above stimulating them by causing a little bit of irritation sometimes. Would our kick-about draw the principal out, thanks to his disapproval of our boisterous behavior?

I stopped contemplating this abruptly when a plastic ball hit me in the face at full speed. For a second, I actually saw stars. From somewhere in the shadows at the opposite end of the gym, I could hear a priest snickering. "Sorry," Stephen chuckled, not sounding remotely sorry at all. I let out a couple of choice expletives, the sort of words that would have earned me a few 'Hail Marys' if I wasn't an agnostic.

No EVPs were recorded during our latest kick-around session, so we decided to carry out a walk-through, checking on the state of things and comparing it to how we had left the school earlier that morning.

As things turned out, none of our equipment had been messed with overnight; everything was just as we had left it, spread out on tables in the break room. Leaving aside the shadow figure that Stephen had seen downstairs in the gym, most of the unusual activity the night before had seemed to come from the upper floors. We agreed that focusing our time and attention up there would be a good way to begin.

While Erik and I checked our equipment, Stephen went upstairs to the theater and set up his spirit box, a device which uses radio frequency-hopping to communicate with discarnate entities — or so some people believe. Others claim what comes out through the speaker on the spirit box is really nothing more than gibberish, the auditory equivalent of pareidolia. I can see it from both sides, because I've experienced both results on multiple occasions — sometimes a voice that is so loud and clear that it is unquestionably intelligent, and at other times a hodge-podge of meaningless drivel. To quote the great American philosopher Forrest Gump, you just never know what you're going to get.

Apparently, nobody was going to talk to Stephen through the box this time. Erik and I, meanwhile, had wandered the halls individually. My phone pinged, indicating an incoming text. It was Stephen.

DID EITHER OF YOU GUYS JUST COME UP HERE AND STICK YOUR HEAD AROUND THE DOOR?

We went up there and assured him that neither of us had been upstairs at all since he had first gone up to the theater. This was odd, because while he was up on the stage fiddling with the settings on his spirit box, Stephen had gotten the distinct impression that somebody was standing behind him.

Turning around, he caught just a glimpse of a dark head and shoulders peeking around the door.

They were shadowy in nature, and while he hadn't really thought that Erik or I were responsible, he felt it necessary to ask anyway. It appeared that somebody was once again taking an interest in him and his activities.

Having traipsed all over the building already, and gotten in close to 5,000 steps (according to my FitBit) none of us really felt like going too far afield just yet.

It was mutually agreed upon that we would stick to the second floor, and check out Mrs. Martin's classroom.

We rigged up a pair of laser microphones in there. This ingenious piece of equipment involved setting up a laser beam that bounced from mirrors, spanning most of the room.

The idea was for any spirit entities that might be present to break the laser beam, introducing their own words or thoughts into it, and thereby creating sound waves that we could hear and interpret. Without even the faintest hint of embarrassment at talking to thin air, Erik raised his voice and explained the way in which the laser mics worked, entreating *somebody* to either speak into the laser beam or to walk right through it.

"We'd like to speak with the Principal, please," I said, adopting my most respectful tone. "Mr. Principal, are you around?"

There was no response whatsoever from the laser mic.

"Are we alone?" Erik asked. "Am I talking to nobody?"

"Hey, that's bad grammar," I smirked. "Is there an English teacher that can come and correct him?"

Still no answer. Oh, the irony.

Sticking to the premise that the third floor was usually the most active, we went up to the auditorium and set up our equipment there. It had yielded some interesting results the night before, and I was hoping that the female who had spoken to me would make her presence known again.

No such luck, unfortunately, although we DID have a great discussion about dead 1980s rock stars, so it wasn't a total loss. The in-depth debate was interrupted by the sound of a thud, once again coming from somewhere out there in the third-floor hallway… the *empty* third-floor hallway.

Stephen began to ask some generalized questions about life in the spirit world. What were conditions like over there? Was there pain? Fatigue? Homes? Vehicles? Education?

Another loud noise came from somewhere outside the auditorium, this one closer than the last. Once again, we couldn't see anybody out there.

Stephen saw what he thought was a shadow figure, dashing quickly past one of the doorways. He began to ask questions about the philosophy and methods of spirit communication, sticking with a theme that seemed to be generating some interest from the spirits of Farrar. Erik saw a streak of light from out in the hallway, one of several that each of us had seen at some point during the night.

I was interested in testing out the theory that there was some kind of portal located outside the principal's office. While Erik and Stephen each went off to find a classroom of their own, I took my tablet over to the principal's office and sat down at the wooden desk. The office was surprisingly small, but not too cramped with just me occupying it.

Flipping open the iPad keyboard and propping it up as a makeshift stand, I dialed down the brightness on the screen as far as it would possibly go. Thanks to the cold glow of the word processor program, I lost some of my night vision, but I gained something I felt was more valuable: the opportunity to write a small part of a book about the haunting of Farrar Elementary while I was actually sitting at the principal's desk inside that same school. This is a tradition that I had started a few years before, and had since grown quite fond of. I rather like the idea that some of the words and sentences you are now reading were first given life inside the building that you are reading about. Although it might take you out of the flow of the narrative for a moment or two, dear reader, rest assured that as these lines were being written, I was peeking over the top of my iPad and gazing out the window of the principal's office, into the blackness of the third-floor hallway at Farrar.

I kept hoping that the huge shadow figure that had been seen by John Tenney and Erik, to name just two, would put in an appearance, particularly if there really *was* a spirit portal located just a few feet in front of me… but alas, it was not to be. Nothing was moving up there on the third floor. There were no further light anomalies, nor were there any more unexplained noises or disembodied footsteps.

Still, one likes to live in hope, and so I sat there, writing out a few notes regarding our experiences so far. I kept on looking out of the window, but nothing came along to disturb me, I am sad to say. I could only hope that wherever they had gone to, my colleagues were having better luck than I was.

Fascinated by the kitchen, Stephen had gone there and set up a laser microphone on the counter, surrounding it with EM pumps. Laser mics work by firing a beam from an emitter to a receiver. It is connected to a speaker. It is possible to speak directly into the beam, and thereby cause the beam to act like a microphone, as the laser has the ability to carry sound.

No sooner had the microphone been set up than a voice came through the speaker that said the words, WHAT IS THIS? It was a male voice, which we found interesting because the kitchen is said to be haunted by the spirit of a lady who worked at the elementary school for more than 30 years, cooking tens of thousands of dinners for children.

The atmosphere felt unnaturally flat, even to somebody like me who has all the psychic sensitivity of a lump of concrete. We tried everything we could think of to stir things up, from EM pumps dumping energy into the air to another game of kick-ball in the gym. No matter what we tried, the mood inside Farrar Elementary felt totally limp.

Daylight wasn't too far off when we walked outside into the cool morning air. Erik locked the doors behind us. Aside from the insects, all was quiet outside Farrar. The evening had been something of an anticlimax, and we were, if the truth be told, just a little disappointed.

It has been said by many that the school, like so many other haunted locations, tends to be a 'feast or famine' experience. On night one, we had gotten the feast. Night two had been the opposite. Now there was just one night left.

Day 3 – E. E. Bensen

After sleeping in a bit, we awoke in our hotel rooms the next morning and proceeded to embark on our usual routine. The first order of business was to find some lunch, and then we'd head over to the school. Upon arrival, I fished the key that Jim had given to me from my pocket, and opened the front door. We spent a few minutes relaxing in the break room before eventually gathering up some equipment and wandering the building individually.

I went down to the gymnasium for a while and sat on the bleachers in silence, taking numerous photos of the area with my full spectrum camera. It was mid-afternoon, and the school was illuminated by the daylight coming in through the windows. I was unsurprised that none of the photos appeared to contain anything remotely resembling paranormal phenomena. After all, I have taken several thousand photos in haunted locations over the years, and to date I have found only one that contains what I believe to be an apparition. It was taken in the gas chamber room at the Museum of Colorado Prisons, and the apparition in question is quite solid and actually blocking the open doorway. That picture is included in my first book, *Supposedly Haunted.*

I walked over to the boiler room and peeked around in there for a few minutes, then headed up to the second floor.

One of the nice things about Farrar, is that all of the classrooms have markings on the chalkboards from previous investigators. These date back in some cases quite a few years, and I always enjoy walking around and reading the signatures and names of the various groups. Littered among these, you can find the names of para-celebrities which are always a fun thing to stumble upon. Once again, I found John Tenney's last name scrawled out in the corner of a board, and in true Tenney-like fashion, it is written upside down. I smiled when I saw it.

Occasionally you can find statements such as "nothing

happened", or, "this is fake" and so on. I just chuckle when I see these, given my past experiences in the school. Still, it is a reminder than the paranormal is fickle in terms of its presentation to any given person or group, or their willingness to accept it.

At 3:08 PM, my pocket vibrated as the mobile phone within alerted me to a text message from Stephen that read this exactly, "Hey, did one of you come up, poke your head in to the theatre and leave?" A reply came from Richard mere seconds later that simply stated, "No."

I wandered up to the auditorium to find Stephen fiddling with some equipment, and he was the only one on the floor. Since I had been near the stairs to the top floor when the text message came in, I didn't bother to reply myself, instead opting to simply go up there and see what was going on. He gestured at the door and again asked, "Did you just poke your head around the corner right there?" I shook my head and smiled while replying, "Nope. Wasn't me."

Richard arrived a few moments later. Stephen proceeded to describe that a very distinct tall figure had literally leaned into the room, presumably to look at him, and then ducked back out of sight when he fully turned his head to see it. The infamous shadow man had apparently decided to make yet another appearance, in broad daylight no less.

About two hours later, Stephen was setting up a laser microphone system in the kitchen area on the first floor. We had not been able to investigate that room in the past given so much stuff was stored in there; however, it had been tidied up somewhat recently.

We have had shocking success with these mics during past investigations, and have had a few instances where completely unexplainable, clear and direct responses to our questions came through the speaker. In this instance, Stephen reported a voice emanating from the speaker immediately after he had turned it on that said, *"What is this?"* Unfortunately, he was still in the middle of setting up and hadn't yet turned on an audio recorder since the voice had appeared so quickly. Still, it is a very cool experience for him, and more proof that the laser mic is a viable tool for investigations.

At one point, I decided to run out to my vehicle to grab the flashlight that I had left in the driver's door pocket the night before, as well as a bottle of water. It would still be daylight for a while, but I wanted to make sure that I had light in case I needed it.

Stephen and Richard were still roaming the school, and as I left the break room area and walked down the main first floor hallway, I decided to leave the audio recorder and speaker I was carrying on the ledge of a window that overlooks the gymnasium. I figured there was no sense in carrying that stuff outside just to bring it right back in. I went outside and retrieved the flashlight and bottle of water, and let myself back into the building. Ensuring that the front door was again locked, I walked down the short hallway to the left of the main staircase that one is presented with upon entering the school, swung open the door, and turning slightly right I headed straight for the window sill where I had left my equipment.

To my right was a set of stairs leading down into the gymnasium, and as I walked diagonally from the door I had just entered to the window overlooking the space, I saw in my peripheral vision that at the bottom of the stairs was standing a completely black but well defined shadow figure. It was very tall, easily close to seven feet, and completely motionless. A single illuminated light bulb on the ceiling was situated just over its head. I stopped dead in my tracks and turned my head rapidly, however once I was staring directly at the area, it was just completely gone with no trace. I turned my head slowly back forward to see if I could still catch a glimpse using my peripheral vision, but I could not. I stood there for a moment gazing at the now empty space at the bottom of the stairs, with a smile slowly forming on my lips and one eyebrow raised.

"Hey, I just saw you down there," I began, "Do you remember me?" The school remained silent. After about a minute I gathered my gear from the window sill, and headed to the top floor. The thought of Stephen's sighting just inside of the door to the boiler room popped into my head. The total distance from where he had seen the shadow figure to where I had just witnessed it again, is no more than perhaps 20 steps. Not to mention his recent sighting in the auditorium.

I arrived on the top floor and proceeded to sit in the Principal's office overlooking the hallway for close to an hour.

The environment was serene overall. I would occasionally hear Stephen or Richard milling around on the floors below, but otherwise nothing happened to speak of.

My initial sighting of the shadow figure a few years prior had happened on the stairs merely a few feet from where I was sitting, so I tried doing a couple of quick EVP sessions and subsequently playing back the recordings immediately through my speaker.

Unfortunately, I captured nothing but my own dumb questions. After growing tired of sitting still for so long, I ventured back down to the break room on the first floor.

I took a seat on the couch facing the open door and could see into the hallway clearly. All was mostly quiet as the others were still wandering about performing experiments and exploration of their own, and I would hear them only occasionally. After a few minutes as I sat there in silence drinking my bottle of water, I realized that attempting to check e-mail from my phone was an exercise in futility... so I gave up and simply stared at the hallway beyond the open door for a few seconds.

Suddenly, moving from right to left, I saw what looked like a slightly oblong soccer ball-sized black shadow pass in front of the door. It was situated just above the floor, semi-transparent, and made no sound. The rate of speed is what I'd call normal walking pace. It was still daylight, and plenty of natural light was coming in from the outside. In addition, the light in the hall was on.

This was not a faint nondescript sighting that can be second-guessed or attributed to any normal occurrence. I was literally staring right at it, and tracked the shadow with my eyes as it crossed in front of the open door. It was three dimensional and moving in the center of the floor.

I jumped to my feet, nearly spilling the bottle of water into my lap in the process, then made my way rapidly to the door. Stepping out into the hallway, there was no trace of the thing whatsoever. I ran up the few stairs to my left to see if it had gone up the main flight of stairs there, but again saw nothing. It was a very strange sighting indeed.

After a few minutes the others joined me in the break room, and we compared notes about our solo experiences before finally deciding to go find some dinner.

About two hours later we returned to the school after dark and prepped for our investigation. I'm disappointed to report that nothing notable whatsoever happened that night in the way of anything paranormal. It would seem as though the school had given all that it was willing to give earlier that day, and also on the previous night. We had a good time anyway and eventually wrapped up in the early hours of the morning and headed back to our hotel. We would have one more shot the following day. Again, I figured that if no other paranormal experiences were to be had, it would be impossible to be unhappy with all the team had experienced up to that point. In many ways, the school had already delivered well beyond what any reasonable investigator could expect over a brief 48-hour period of time

Chapter Four

Day 4 – Richard Estep

Prior to heading back to Farrar for our third and final night, we enjoyed a very convivial meal with Will and his wife.

While we were talking about our mixed bag of experiences over the past couple of days, Will gave us some very pointed and straightforward advice.

"In my experience, the best way to get results in there is to not try too hard," he said. "If you go in with a bunch of gizmos with flashing lights and strange noises, you'll probably get nothing. Forget about collecting evidence: it doesn't work that way inside the school a lot of the time. Just go in with a notepad and an open mind. Be ready to experience what the school is ready to give you, and forget about trying to record it."

In other words: we were advised to stick with the old school approach (pun very much intended) as much as we possibly could. That made good sense to us. To this day, we all agree that the paranormal research field has gotten overly reliant on gadgets, which are often more of a distraction than they are a help. The original 'ghost hunters' — men of great renown such as Sir Oliver Lodge, Sir William Crookes, and Sir Arthur Conan Doyle — made do with the most rudimentary equipment, preferring to use the most basic kit and their own five senses...six, if you include common sense.

After Will and his wife had left, we decided to take his advice to heart. "Split up," he had told us, using the rationale that we were less likely to crowd the spirits that way. I couldn't help but think that on the flip side of the coin, it would also make us all a little more vulnerable.

I went to the principal's office again, but this time, rather than write, I simply sat on the steps and stared out into the darkness of the third-floor hallway.

Stephen chose the gymnasium, and Erik settled himself down in a classroom on the second floor.

We sat in silence for an hour. There was nothing creepy about the atmosphere inside the school that night. The air didn't feel particularly charged. All was peaceful, mirroring the second night more than the first. When the clock struck midnight (and just how perfect was *that?*) we all met up again. Erik and I had nothing to report, but for Stephen, things had been considerably less quiet.

"Did you guys hear screaming?" Stephen asked, the minute I walked through the door of the break room.

"What kind of screaming?"

"A woman's voice, really loud and high-pitched."

Erik and I shook our heads. We hadn't heard a thing.

"That's strange," Stephen said, wearing an expression of puzzlement. "I heard it as clear as day."

The acoustics inside the school were such that no matter where we had been, with the possible exception of the deepest recesses of the boiler room, a scream should have been audible from just about anywhere.

"Any idea where it came from?" Erik wanted to know.

"Sounded like it was upstairs."

Which should have been impossible. Erik and I had both been located upstairs, and therefore were much closer to the source of the screaming than Stephen had been.

Had it been a natural scream, we should have heard it much more clearly than the priest had.

I wondered aloud if it could have been an animal cry coming from outside — foxes can sound a lot like humans screaming, particularly when they're mating — but Stephen was adamant that it had come from somewhere up above his head.

Curiouser and curiouser.

We went back upstairs and set up the laser mics up there, hoping to communicate with whoever it was that Stephen thought he had heard. Stephen adjusted the red laser beam's orientation with painstaking care and precision, until the sound of the signal coming through the speaker was constant. While he was doing this, Erik and I dispersed a series of EMF sensors in an array around the room, in the hope of giving us early warning of any unseen guests. For the next few hours, we tried our best to make contact with the spirits of Farrar, using almost every trick in the book…

…all to no avail.

We had deliberately chosen to leave spirit boards off the menu, out of deference to the location itself. It had been speculated on *Ghost Stalkers* that the use of such a board might have sparked some of the more aggressive activity at Farrar, and while I personally believe that such devices are no more dangerous than any other tool that is intended to be used for spirit communication, we didn't want to worry Jim and Nancy by using one in what is basically their home.

We looked at one another, each of us thinking the same thing.

Outside, the sky was getting lighter. The birds were starting to sing.

We were out of time.

The three of us packed all of our equipment away in cases, policed up our trash, and took one last walk through the school.

The classrooms, hallways, and gymnasium were all quiet. The sense of vague unease that we'd all sensed two nights before was gone, replaced by a placid sense of calm.

Sometimes, when you're investigating a haunted location, you somehow become instinctively aware that the activity has dried up for the night.

You just *know*.

There will be no more knocks, footsteps, disembodied voices or EVPs. It's almost as if the building is done with you. The resident entities have given you as much of their time and attention as you are going to get, and you should be grateful for whatever it was that you were given.

It's something that we just have to learn to accept.

Even the auditorium felt inert. I went up onto the stage one last time, turning to look out into the huge room. There were no shadow figures lurking on the periphery that I could see.

I won't say that I could have curled up in that easy chair and gone to sleep, but there was no feeling of being watched any longer. In its prime, Farrar Elementary had been a bustling place, with the laughter of children echoing throughout its walls.

Many paranormal investigators have experienced the locker doors slamming themselves shut, seemingly of their own volition. They remained resolutely silent as we walked past them. I looked up at the principal's office. No shadowy Principal stood looking back at me. If the Janitor or the Librarian were present, they too were keeping out of our way. Perhaps, I reasoned, they were sick of our company after three nights, and wanted nothing more than for us to leave them in peace.

They were about to get their wish.

I have read a lot of paranormal non-fiction books. I have also watched literally hundreds of episodes of para-'reality' TV shows and documentary movies. Almost all of them have one thing in common.

The activity always seems to peak at the end.

From the perspective of somebody editing a TV show, that makes complete sense. Ideally, you want to keep the audience on the edge of their seats, constantly wondering just where the next scare is going to come from. The activity builds and builds, before finally peaking at the climax of the episode. It's a tried and tested formula, and in terms of TV viewership, it works, which is why so many of these shows look the same. (A big tip of the hat to *Ghost Stalkers, Ghost Lab,* and *Paranormal Lockdown*, who didn't necessarily play that game). After all, nobody wants to tune in for 45 minutes to an hour, only to be rewarded with an anticlimax at the end.

The same is true of many books, perhaps the most famous of them being Jay Anson's multi-million-dollar bestseller, *The Amityville Horror*. Most of the exciting stuff comes at the end.

Our books aren't structured that way, for one very important reason: real life doesn't work like that. This is reality, not Hollywood. When paranormal investigators conduct research in the field over the space of several days, all too often the case can peak on the first or second day, and then decline steadily afterward. There is no equivalent to the magic of TV editing for the writer, unless he or she is willing to bend the facts in order to fit their narrative — and once you set foot on that slippery slope, the chances are that your credibility will suffer somewhere along the way.

Most field research is slow, boring, and yields little in the way of results. Eighty to ninety percent of the investigator's time is wasted, though what's left is usually well worth the cost.

During our three days at Farrar Elementary, the school was most active on the first night. Despite our best efforts, the level of paranormal activity dwindled over the course of the next two days. Sometimes, that's just how it is. That's not to say that there weren't flashes of pure wonder. I will go to my grave remembering the feeling of stunned awe that hit me when I heard the female voice answering me from somewhere up on the third floor.

Stephen and Erik will go to theirs without ever have gotten tired of imitating my facial expression from that same, golden moment.

We had heard disembodied voices (and, in Stephen's case, screaming), witnessed shadow figures and light anomalies. That single, crystal-clear response, spoken in an unseen woman's voice, had more than justified the entire experience for me. It was, and I suspect shall forever remain, the single most impressive piece of paranormal voice phenomena that I will ever be fortunate enough to witness.

We refuse to exaggerate or embellish what happened to us at Farrar, even if it means that this book does not follow the traditional format. This is the truth of paranormal investigation, the unvarnished reality of it, and we respect our readers too much to pretend otherwise.

But the story of Farrar Elementary is a fascinating one, and during our quest to uncover the secrets of this haunted old school, we tracked down some of those who have had incredible, almost unbelievable experiences within those walls.

While our part in this tale may be over, rest assured that this story of haunted high strangeness is far from finished...

Day 4 – E. E. Bensen

We returned to the school the following day, and again experienced nothing of interest during our daytime investigations.

After several hours of attempting in vain to contact anything paranormal, we ran out of EVP questions that would be able to be used among mixed company, and decided to take a dinner break.

Our questions always slowly degrade into some pretty hilarious and outlandish scenarios, and this was no different. Theorizing that perhaps inviting a few people who are intimately familiar with the school might help to stir something up, we invited Will Conkel and his wife Jacquelyn to investigate with us that night. After all, they had been married on the stage in the auditorium a few years prior.

Upon arrival at the school after dinner, we asked our guests where they would like to investigate. Without hesitation, both indicated that the best place was always the top floor, and in particular, the auditorium. I can't dispute that myself as some of the things I've experienced in the school during past investigations did indeed happen in that area, however I'll note for the prospective future visitor that we have had strange things happen everywhere in the building overall.

We entered the pitch-black auditorium, and almost immediately, a few of us heard what sounded like a disembodied woman's voice. I couldn't make out what it said, but it seemed like a few syllables to me. I have no explanation for that, and it does correlate to the female voice that responded to us on the first night. It would seem as though whoever she is, she has mastered the ability to be heard by us decidedly fleshier folks. We each found a seat in various sections of the room, and chatted for a good long while about the paranormal in general. It became clear immediately that while all of us come from very diverse backgrounds and walks of life that we are of the same paranormal family, or tribe, if you will.

One of the greatest things about the field is that it can sometimes bring together people in this way. We tend to seek each other out, and upon finding fellow paranormal kin, there is an unspoken bond that is formed. Some of the best people I've ever met in my life were introduced to me in this exact way. We'd surely have never crossed paths otherwise.

After having spent so much time in the school, Will and Jacquelyn were not surprisingly full of stories regarding their experiences at Farrar. I couldn't really take any notes, nor did I care to do so at that moment, but I think I can relay a few of them with reasonable accuracy. At one point they described how the auditorium can sometimes become "darker than dark", and even appear to have a misty swirling vortex within it. This immediately resonated with Stephen and I after the weird visual experience we had two days prior. I still want to say that it was just my eyes playing tricks in an exceedingly dark room; however, I cannot dispute the correlation with Stephen experiencing the same thing at the same time, combined with this new information.

Will indicated that the auditorium may be the location of a portal of some kind, a place where the supernatural intersects with our reality and can pass between the two worlds seamlessly. I can neither confirm nor deny this, and I don't really know how I feel about the theory in general, other than to say that I am open to it.

The paranormal field is so chock full of high strangeness that it becomes pretty much impossible to discredit any given theory or belief. I've come to the conclusion that it is really up to the individual in terms of what concepts he or she is willing to wrap their mind around. All that I can say about it is that it's endlessly intriguing.

Another story the couple related to us was that of what seemed to be an apparition, sitting on the edge of the stage. In that case, the room was again dark, and over a period of time the thing became slowly visible. It took a while for the people present to acknowledge it, as surely some did not believe their eyes at first, much like Stephen and I a few days prior. If I recall correctly, Will indicated that eventually he couldn't stand the urge anymore and flipped on a light, only to find that the ghostly figure had vanished. This is one of the great frustrations with the field of paranormal investigation. One moment something is present and tangible, and the next moment it is gone without a trace. Our memories and visualizations are usually all that remain after. In the end, we have to accept these as the primary reward for our exhaustive efforts.

These days, however, that is good enough for me. I no longer try to prove the existence of the paranormal to anyone, I just try to have an experience, and then share that experience with anyone who might be interested. As soon as I took that point of view years ago, my search for the unknown became far more enjoyable.

Jacquelyn and Will related another experience where the tall shadow figure often seen in the school presented itself by standing in the doorway of the auditorium on one dark night. As it stood there motionless for a long period of time, Will decided to try and get a closer look. He approached it slowly as it remained steadfast and unmoving. Finally, he got to within feet of it, then stood there staring eye to… whatever, probably eye, in a rare and prolonged paranormal encounter. Usually, these things are there one minute, and gone the next, so was is quite intriguing to me. He reported that after some period of time, the figure suddenly lunged at him in what he described as an almost elastic or rubber band effect. In other words, it shot forward at unbelievable speed and stretched out so as to be right up into his face, then recoiled back just as quickly.

Will's response to this action was to laugh, which I found quite odd. I'm guessing that most people would have had to make a late- night trip to Walmart for clean underwear, but not him. Will seems to be one of the few people who have no fear of the school's paranormal inhabitants, or the shadow man in particular. While I can't say that I am fearful of that entity myself, given that my interactions have been somewhat innocuous thus far, I will openly admit that I probably would have been making the regrettable drive to Walmart had this experience happened to me.

During our visit, Will relayed a theory about the shadow man that was presented to him by John Tenney. I'll do my best to paraphrase. In satisfyingly Tenney-esque fashion, he theorized that the shadow man might actually be a future deceased (or not, to make it even stranger) version of the Will Conkel we have today. This somewhat blew my mind, as it was not something that I'd have come up with myself. Of course, one's initial reaction to this theory might be to dismiss it readily. I might have considered doing that myself; however, there are a few things that I could not deny.

Will is the caretaker of the school, and loves the building in a way that few people do. He is self-admittedly drawn to it in some strange, hard-to-define way. The shadow man is generally slender, just like Will. Based on my sightings, I would estimate it to be at least 6 foot 7 inches tall, just like Will. Lastly, Will is (strangely enough) not afraid of the shadow man to an extent that I would assert is well beyond what any other given brave person would be. I'd like to think that Stephen, Richard, and I are pretty bold when it comes to investigating the paranormal, but I don't believe for a second that any of us could have had the same experience as Will had, without having our hearts seriously tested in the process. It is an interesting theory to be sure.

Eventually, Will and Jacquelyn headed home, leaving us to investigate for a few hours before beginning our journey back to Denver the following day.

Again, the school was extremely quiet overall. We split up and roamed its classrooms and hallways solo for a while. To my recollection, Richard spent some time on the top floor, and situated himself in the principal's office. Stephen roamed the second floor for a bit and I believe may have explored the gymnasium as well.

I sat in the break room for a while, and all was relatively quiet. Eventually I wandered into the kitchen area for a few minutes, then began roaming the main hall, and finally the gymnasium on the bottom floor. I didn't experience anything paranormal, but I'll admit that I lacked the overall fortitude to stay in the boiler room alone for very long. I recall walking into the small connecting room off the gym, flashlight in hand, and arriving at the boiler room door. I slowly opened it and peered inside. All was serene, or at least, as serene as a creepy room like that could ever be.

After a few tentative steps, the sound of the door closing me behind me got my heart rate going for a few seconds. It is at times like these that I have to wonder as a paranormal researcher why we do things like that to ourselves. I clicked off my flashlight and stood there in the murky blackness for what was probably only two or three minutes, then retreated back out to the more inviting main gymnasium area. I will occasionally test myself like that, but I'm not sure why. Perhaps it is just to prove to myself that I still have what it takes, or, maybe I'm just weird.

After sitting on the bleachers for a few minutes, I stood and began to survey the area with my flashlight. A slight pang of sadness struck me that we were close to wrapping up our three-day visit to Farrar, and I had no idea when I might be back again. I still don't, so perhaps I should work on fixing that and put another visit on the calendar for the future. I made my way back to the break room and sat in my usual spot on the couch, facing the door.

Ten minutes later, Stephen appeared and asked excitedly if I had heard an extremely loud scream on the second floor where he had just been investigating by himself. I looked at him perplexed and replied that I most certainly had not. There would be no way to not hear such a thing almost anywhere in the building, let alone where I was stationed right at the bottom of the stairs.

A few minutes later we heard Richard making his way down from the third floor, and again Stephen asked him the same question.

He had also heard nothing out of the ordinary, and reported the third floor as being very quiet and unassuming during his solo investigation.

We have no idea how such a pronounced scream heard by Stephen could be missed by the two of us, so that remains an unanswered question. There are a few theories that simply get weirder the deeper down the rabbit hole you go. Could he have heard it psychically somehow? Meaning, it was projected into his thoughts by an unseen force or entity. Who knows for sure? I will say that I have had that experience a few times in my life, as documented in my other books, so I know firsthand that it is indeed quite possible.

We wrapped our investigation, and on the window sill overlooking the gymnasium I left the key to the building and a copy of my most recent book containing a chapter on Farrar for the owners to find in the morning. Last in line, I quietly slipped out the front door, and ensured that it was securely locked behind me. I placed one hand on its cold metal surface, paused for a moment, and quietly whispered, "See ya later."

Chapter Five
Day 5 – E. E. Bensen

One more night of investigation lay ahead of us. When planning the trip several months prior, I had noted that the infamous Villisca Ax Murder house was (almost) on the way home, and it would be a shame to just simply drive past.

It didn't take any convincing at all for Stephen and Richard to agree to stop there.

We arrived at around four o'clock in the afternoon, paid our fees, and were given two sets of keys. This was to be the third visit for Stephen and I, and Richard's first. (AAPI first visited Villisca on August 28, 2014).

There were only three investigators during that trip as well, and we were treated to what remains to this day, one of the most violent thunderstorms I've ever witnessed. It just couldn't have been any better in terms of a real-life horror movie scenario, and we were absolutely thrilled. We also collected more EVP audio evidence that night than we have ever captured on any single investigation in our history. I believe the total count was something like 27 EVPs. These were listened to by all three present, and were agreed to be of paranormal origin, and I'll point out that we threw away just as many that were not able to be verified and cross-checked on multiple recorders.

Under normal circumstances, we are lucky to capture one good EVP, if any, from any given investigation. A great evidence haul would be a few to perhaps six EVPs, so this was truly extraordinary. I'm not really sure why that was, but it almost certainly must have had to do with the highly charged electrical environment created by the storm. Additionally, we heard a few disembodied voices and captured some on the audio recorders.

There were no overtly paranormal experiences however, such as seeing anomalies with our eyes, in photos, or whatnot. On a subsequent visit in March of 2016 literally nothing happened, and we got no EVP audio evidence either. As such, Stephen and I weren't quite sure what to expect on our third visit. It seemed to us that it could easily go either way.

We ended up hanging out in the living room of the small house for a while, until finally a knock came at the door. I had the best vantage point and quickly recognized the epic beard belonging to Johnny Houser standing on the porch. We had notified him that we'd be investigating the house, and he lives very close by. Johnny is generally regarded as "Mr. Villisca" after having been involved in the operations of the house for quite some time. I had never met him in person before, having only seen him on TV and VIDI Space shows a few times, so it was cool to be able to do so.

Within just seconds of Johnny entering the house, we were rewarded with a very loud bang in the living room, mere feet from where we stood in the kitchen. It sounded very much to me like a laptop or something similar had slid off the couch somehow and crashed to the floor. However, upon inspection, we could find absolutely nothing out of place. It would seem as though the Villisca Ax Murder house was saying "hello" to its old friend Johnny. He was not the least bit surprised by this, which in turn, didn't surprise us either. Things were looking promising for the night that lay ahead.

After sitting with Johnny for a while and chatting about various things paranormal, he headed back home, and we eventually set about our investigation for the night. I placed a device called a Paramid on the floor in the upstairs bedroom. This is an ultrasonic motion sensing device with about a four-foot range to either side of it, and LED sensors to indicate which side motion is being detected on, and how far away the "object" might be. I've used this thing numerous times, and it does sometimes go off inexplicably, however it has never led me to believe that it produces false positives easily.

After setting out more gizmos with strange names, we sat in the living room again, and almost immediately the Paramid alerted us with a couple of beeps. Over the course of a few minutes, it continued to do so, but the interval was not consistent. We thought that perhaps the batteries were dying or something, however I don't think that was necessarily the case given my extensive past experience with it. That had never happened before.

At one point, Stephen headed upstairs to try and turn on the heater that is located in that same bedroom, which would have put him five to six feet from the Paramid. It was behind him, and didn't alert initially when he went up there. After a few seconds of fiddling with the controls on the heater unit, without success in turning it on, he reported hearing a footstep and shuffling noise behind him and the Paramid immediately sounded its motion sensing alarm. Naturally, he didn't see anything.

We observed several instances of the Paramid alarming upstairs, while we were sitting in the living room, and after some discussion, I went up and retrieved the device and replaced the eight AA batteries. I placed it right back where it had been before, and noted that it seemed to be slightly more sensitive to motion with fresh power running to it, however I'll point out that it detected me reaching down to pick it up with the old batteries as well.

Over the course of the night, it went off only one or two more times, leaving us with sufficient evidence to at least doubt its earlier performances. I can't say that it was anything paranormal setting the device off, but I will say that the behavior was not consistent with past investigations, and Stephen actually hearing something behind him before the alarm went off, is certainly intriguing. If anything sums up paranormal investigation, it can be said that it is certainly an endeavor in analyzing false positives.

Stephen placed one of his flashlights into an old candle holder on the wall in the living room to give us some ambient light. The bulb was red and thereby cast a satisfyingly eerie glow over the room and the various photos on the walls. After a short time, the light suddenly went off completely. The natural assumption was that the batteries had died, although Stephen indicated that they were fresh and that it was an LED light, meaning that it lasts basically until you feel like you should change the batteries due to age whether they need it or not.

Someone said something to the effect of, "If that was you, can you turn the light back on?" Much to our surprise, the light came back on instantly.

I'd like to point out that this flashlight has a button on the end of it that has a very tactile feel, and requires some pressure to actuate. It has three modes: off, on, and flash. Over the course of the next several minutes, we were able to consistently get the flashlight to change modes on command in response to questions. I would say that the success rate was at least 90%. Normally I'd assume this was simple coincidence; however, I have to concede that the behavior was well outside anything that could be easily explained away. Not to mention the fact that there really was no reason for it to do such a thing; it had never done so in the past, according to Stephen. He changed the batteries anyway, and put a different flashlight in its place for a while. That one behaved just fine; however, when we put the original one back up in the candle holder, it again responded a few times, exactly on demand, before seeming to become bored with the whole endeavor, and remaining illuminated for the rest of the night. Of course, I can't say for sure that what happened with the flashlight was paranormal, but in our considerable investigation experience, it was notable, at the very least. Personally, I feel that there were too many instances of it behaving on command when it came to selecting the flashing versus constant-on modes to call the behavior purely coincidental.

We eventually packed our gear and headed back to the hotel. It had been a long five days of paranormal investigation, and all of us were quite tired and in search of much needed rest at that point. In the morning, we packed up the vehicle and pointed the navigation system back to Richard's house. It had been a good trip, and I felt as though we had accomplished our mission of gathering evidence to write this book that you are reading now.

Chapter Six

Richard Estep:
Interview with Sarah Stream

When she isn't busy raising a family or working in her chosen field of dentistry, Sarah Stream is an avid paranormal investigator. Her ghost-hunting beat is usually roaming around the state of Iowa, particularly the abandoned former nursing home that is now known as Malvern Manor.

It was the summer of 2018, and Sarah seized upon the opportunity to investigate the Farrar School during their two-day 'Detention at Farrar' event, a chance for members of the public to spend forty-eight hours roaming those haunted hallways and attempt to uncover some of its mysteries for themselves.

It was early on Friday morning when she parked her car outside the school. As she had driven up the long driveway, the imposing edifice had seemed to speak to her, promising a weekend full of adventure and intrigue.

Will Conkel was outside, working hard to get things squared away in advance of the event's opening. It was shaping up to be a particularly hot July, and Will was, in Sarah's own words, 'sweating his ass off.' Glad of a reason to take a break, Will welcomed Sarah warmly and opened up the school for her. She decided to spend a little time wandering about the place, peeking into the empty classrooms and seeing where each hallway and staircase led. Once she had gotten a feel for the building, Sarah went back outside and volunteered to help Will set things up.

While they were talking, another car rolled up outside the school. A young lady got out, accompanied by her father. Just eleven years old, Madison Smith had already been investigating haunted locations for longer than many adults. Sarah and Madison would spend the afternoon hanging out with one another, and soon developed a strong bond.

As the day wore on, more and more people began to trickle in; people such as Coyote Chris Sutton, a man well-acquainted with the school, Josh Heard (owner of Malvern Manor and a respected investigator in his own right), Jonah Jones, and Will's wife, Jacquelyn.

The field of paranormal investigation has a dark side, one that has nothing to do with spirit entities or energies. It is an ugly truth that far too many para-groups are extremely territorial, seeming to take an almost perverse delight in backstabbing and undermining their fellow groups whenever the opportunity presents itself. All of this in-fighting and politicking serves only to give the field a bad name.

But in Iowa, things are refreshingly different. An attitude of friendly camaraderie exists between the owners and principal investigators of such locations as the Farrar School, Villisca Ax Murder House, and Malvern Manor. You are every bit as likely to find Johnny Houser prowling the hallways at Malvern Manor as you are to find Josh Heard conducting an investigation at Farrar. This is the way it ought to be, and many members of the paranormal scene would do well in taking a leaf out of Iowa's book. The mutual support and cooperation that exists there is truly inspiring.

As day gave way to night, Coyote Chris led everybody in a Native American ceremony, the intent of which was to commune with the energy of an old tree that stood in front of the school. He called upon the spirits of the trees and the surrounding land to dance with those who were gathered at the Farrar School that night, inviting them to be a part of the event.

When the ceremony had concluded, everybody split up into small groups (some went solo) and wandered off, following Chris's instructions to roam around the lands surrounding the school and attempt to feel the energies there and open themselves up to interaction with the spirits.

For some reason, Sarah felt herself drawn to the woods at the southern edge of the property. Making her way over there, she found a dry creek bed and not a lot else.

Looking back the way she had come, she saw that twenty or so people were still encircling the old tree. That was perfect.

She was a bit of a lone wolf when it came to paranormal investigating, and liked the idea of getting away from the crowd in order to do her own thing.

Sarah walked barefoot, something she often liked to do, not only when visiting a haunted place but also during her personal life. She found that it gave her some sort of connection with the earth itself, helping to ground her in a way that was hard to explain.

This far away from the lights of the school, the grounds were completely dark. She stood there silently in the dark, feeling herself breathe and attuning herself to the natural environment that surrounded her. Apart from the low rumble of chattering that came from the group surrounding the tree, everything was still and quiet.

Sarah waited for her eyes to adjust to the darkness, opening herself up spiritually to whatever energies might be around her that night.

Then the shadows began to move. It was subtle at first, beginning as flashes of movement out of the corner of her eye.

Before long, the motion was more blatant. She spent a lot of time working in dark and near-dark conditions, and knew what it was like when your eyes began playing tricks on you.

This wasn't that. These movements were distinct, something more than the interplay of dim light and shadow. Something was out there with her, among the trees.

Despite that, she wasn't the least bit frightened. Part of that was because she usually didn't *get* frightened when strange things happened to her in the darkness. She simply wasn't wired that way. But at the same time, Sarah had begun to sense a certain feeling of playfulness as she stood there at the edge of the grounds. It was almost as if an unseen somebody was enjoying her company and wanted to let her know that she was welcome to be there.

Suddenly she heard footsteps in the middle distance, somewhere behind her. They were coming closer. Sarah turned to look, thinking that it might be a fellow visitor coming to join her. She waited as the footsteps drew nearer, peering out into the darkness.

There was nobody there.

Sarah smiled. This was why she had made the journey to Farrar in the first place. She had only been there for a few hours, and had already been rewarded with the sound of disembodied footsteps. The school was like that, she knew; she had heard that from other paranormal investigators. It was unpredictable, but more often than not, being open to the spirits of the Farrar School meant that they would make their presence known to you, sometimes in the most blatant manner possible.

She felt something pull gently on the hair at the back of her neck. The sensation was subtle but undeniable. Strands of hair were getting tugged on, not forcefully enough to hurt, but firmly enough that the sensation was distinct. This time, Sarah didn't need to turn around to know that there was nobody back there — physically, at least.

Gradually, people began to wander over in her general direction. Wanting to enjoy her solitude for a while longer,

Sarah elected to head on over to the north side, away from the main body of visitors. Finding a secluded spot, she lay down in the grass, folded her arms behind her head, and stared up into the night sky.

It was a crystal-clear night, and she was content just to be in a special place and to stargaze for a while. Before long, something caught her eye.

It was a light, moving quickly from southwest to northeast across the sky, faster than an airplane would travel. In a moment, it was gone.

Whether a satellite passing overhead or something else, it is impossible to say for sure, but looking back on it months afterward, Sarah is convinced that it was a UFO of some kind.

There was to be no formal investigation that first night. After the visitors had wandered around the grounds for a while, they went their separate ways. School was out for the evening, but detention would convene again the next day.

Day two started early. The day was set up as a conference, offering people the opportunity to attend workshops and classes on a diverse range of subjects that spanned the paranormal spectrum. In the afternoon, Will led everybody on a walking tour of the land surrounding the school, expounding on the history and what was known of those who had once lived there.

As the afternoon tour came to a close, the attendees could see that storm clouds were gathering off to the northwest. Thunder rumbled, and jagged forks of lightning speared the ground. Ever the photographer, Sarah decided to take a stroll out into the fields in order to take a few pictures.

After capturing a few lightning strikes, she returned to the school. It was getting dark, and a full night of paranormal investigation beckoned.

Although not a big fan of working in big groups, this particular event was open to the public, and so Sarah fell in with the smallest bunch of people she could find and followed along…for a while, at least. By the time they reached the third floor, she felt something drawing her toward the auditorium, so she snuck away from the main body of people and went to take a look for herself.

Unlike every other classroom up on the third floor, the huge room was surprisingly empty and dark. Quietly, Sarah made her way to the main stage and took a seat on the edge.

What followed was one of the most spiritual and surreal experiences of her entire career as a paranormal investigator. Although everything was still inside the auditorium itself, outside was a different story.

A thunderstorm raged with all the intensity of an artillery barrage, the bass rumble of rolling thunder accompanied by flashes of lightning that lit up the room in stark white brilliance, casting long shadows across the floor.

Every once in a while, the lightning would flare and Sarah would catch sight of a shadow figure moving across some part of the auditorium. She developed the firm conviction that she wasn't in there alone. Her shadowy companions were constantly in motion, never in the same place twice.

After a few minutes, she could hear footsteps coming in through the main doorway. This time, they belonged to a physical person — a gentleman named Nick, who belonged to a different paranormal research group. He walked across to the stage and sat next to Sarah, joining her in her vigil.

The two investigators sat and talked quietly in hushed tones, occasionally raising their voices to make themselves heard over the growling of the thunder. A digital audio recorder was running, though its value was questionable at best thanks to the soundtrack provided by Mother Nature, and a Parascope detector, but they had deployed no other equipment. Somehow it felt to them as if this was the sort of night they were meant to *experience*, not to record.

Light anomalies began to flit across the room, tiny flashes that were gone almost as quickly as they appeared. This is a phenomenon that the authors of this book also experienced in the auditorium at Farrar, along with the other members of their team. Unfortunately, by the time a camera could be readied to take a picture, the lights had disappeared.

The two investigators sat there and called out the things that they were seeing to one another. During one particularly bright flash of lightning, both Sarah and Nick distinctly saw the shadowy outline of a human form, standing next to a chair against the western wall.

"This is one of the best personal experiences I've ever had as a paranormal investigator," Sarah recalls, looking back a few months later. "All we did was experience the building and the storm as it was happening all around us. It was sublime."

The authors of this book agree with Sarah. Sometimes it is all too easy to get caught up in the gadgetry and gizmos aspect of paranormal field research, getting distracted by the latest high-end SLS cameras and bespoke electromagnetic sensing devices that are now on the market. But the truth of the matter is that while equipment definitely has its place, there is a great deal to be said for simply *experiencing* a haunted location. Arguably the best 'ghost detector' out there — if such a thing exists — is the human body itself.

Sarah's experiences at the Farrar School parallel those of many other visitors. Disembodied footsteps, shadow figures, and light anomalies are all common phenomena in this haunted old school.

Chapter Seven
Richard Estep:
Interview with John Tenney

In our opinion, the TV show *Ghost Stalkers* died — if you will excuse the pun — before its time.

Produced by *Ghost Adventures'* Nick Groff, the show featured the unlikely pairing of John Tenney and Chad Lindberg.

Whereas John was more than familiar with the ins and outs of paranormal investigation, Chad had no such background, being best-known as a Hollywood actor in such movies as *The Fast and the Furious,* and such TV shows as (appropriately enough) *Supernatural.*

So, what did these two men have in common? Both had undergone near death experiences at some point in their lives, and were interested in finding out more about the possibility of life after death. This would be accomplished by visiting sites across the United States that were believed to host spirit portals.

When they step foot inside a haunted location, both had a distinctly feline vibe about them, by which we mean that John was one cool cat, and Chad was more like a cat on a hot tin roof. The format of the show meant that each spent one night inside a supposedly haunted location — alone — while the other monitored them from outside the building. Their time at Farrar Elementary yielded some fascinating results.

John was no stranger to Farrar, having investigated and lectured there in the past. He described there being essentially two aspects to the haunting. One was the presence of children, who seemed happy and playful. The other was what he called "dark entities that are willing to pretty much do anything they can to get you out of the building."

He also asks the question that has stumped so many paranormal investigators who are familiar with the old school. With its apparently benign history, why should there be dark, potentially negative activity taking place there now?

Chad Lindberg floats the idea that the close proximity to the town cemetery may be the answer. While this is certainly possible (at least, it may be a contributory factor) we feel it is unlikely to explain the intensity of some of the phenomena taking place at Farrar. There is no shortage of haunted locations that sit next to cemeteries. One of our favorites, the former Tooele Valley Hospital in Utah, is a great example, and the resident investigators believe that spirits from the cemetery drop in from time to time and make their presence known. But those entities are responsible for a relatively small amount of the paranormal activity taking place inside the walls of the old hospital, and we suspect that the same would be true at Farrar. The cemetery at Farrar is also extremely small in comparison to most others, a reflection of the small population size in the town itself.

Johnny Houser, caretaker of and acknowledged expert on the haunted Villisca Ax Murder House, ventures his opinion that there is a ghostly principal who 'gets control of everything,' and has a low tolerance for disorder and chaotic activity inside the school.

It's fair to say that Johnny is a strong guy, not the sort of fellow that would be easy to push around. Early on in this episode, he relates a rather disturbing experience that took place on one of the upper floors. Standing there in the hallway and basically minding his own business, he suddenly felt something take hold of his head and slam it backwards into one of the coat hooks that are mounted on a strip running along the wall. He was extremely lucky not to have sustained a serious injury, such as a fractured skull or even a broken neck.

The message seems clear: *Get the hell out of my school*!

A similar experience was caught on film by investigator Lisa Kovanda, who was sitting inside the library when she felt something push her from beneath her shoulders and thrust her into the air, hurling her an estimated six feet across the room. It seems like no coincidence that she was in the middle of a spirit board session at the time, one in which the unseen communicator had just spelled the words GET OUT.

As with everybody else, Lisa can offer no concrete explanation for the cause of the negative activity at Farrar. Owner Nancy Oliver ascribes Lisa's frightening experience to her having used a spirit board inside the school, which may or may not be the case, but in any eventuality, we believe that the answer is more complex than that.

Tenney believes that there is a portal at Farrar, a doorway which is allowing negative entities to gain access to the school. If his theory is correct, then it would go a long way toward explaining why the school is haunted despite the fact that its history seems to be a mostly pleasant and ordinary one.

So far, we had gotten just five minutes into the episode. John Tenney had already advanced a credible theory that might explain the haunting of the school, and two paranormal investigators had reported violent experiences that made us both a little concerned for our safety when we investigated Farrar for ourselves.

Next, owner Nancy Oliver takes Chad and John on a guided tour of the school, focusing on the hotspots of paranormal activity. They begin down in the basement, where the current school caretaker, Will, saw the tall shadow figure that has been nicknamed 'the Principal.' Nor is he the only person to have encountered this entity, for it is the same spirit that Johnny Houser referred to as liking to have control over the entire school.

According to Nancy, a visiting psychic was scratched across her back when she ventured down into the basement. We made a note to spend some time down there and see if we could replicate their experiences.

Nancy then led them up to the third floor, and talked about the first ghostly experiences that she and her husband, Jim, had when they moved into the school. The sound of children playing, footsteps running through the hallway, and finally the apparitions of little girls were all seen up there, close to the stage in what is now known as 'the auditorium.'

Finally, the *piece de resistance:* what John refers to as 'the most dreaded room in the school'…the principal's office, which Nancy says is the most active part of the school. She cautions them that the Principal has no hesitation in being aggressive if he feels the need to be.

They bring in electrical engineer David Rountree to offer his perspective. This brings in an interesting angle. John and Chad are interested in just how much of the Farrar haunting is driven by the presence of the human investigators themselves, and want to try to gather some data to that effect. David tells them that he is going to hook Chad up to a heart monitor in order to see how his cardiovascular system reacts to being inside the old schoolhouse.

Sticking with the same medical theme, David demonstrates the way in which John is going to wear a brain wave monitor, a device which will send electro-encephalogram (EEG) readings to David via Bluetooth.

The rationale for gathering this medical data is to see how much of what takes place over the next 48 hours is actually being influenced by Chad and John themselves, biologically speaking, and how much of it is their own central nervous systems reacting to the events taking place all around them. The concept is a fascinating one, although speaking as a medical professional, I (Richard) believe that it might be next to impossible to tell which of the two possibilities might be the truth, based purely upon the vital signs alone.

Chad is the first to go. His blood pressure is already running higher than would be considered normal for his age and body type, and his heart beat is tachycardic at a rate of 131 per minute (unless he just pounded a couple of energy drinks or sprinted around the block, it should be somewhere around half that at rest). David Rountree states that the building is already beginning to affect Chad, which — from a psychogenic point of view, is almost certainly the case.

It has to be noted that throughout the season of *Ghost Stalkers*, he shows himself to consistently be the more nervous of the two investigators. Chad is, as he very openly admits, *"extremely uncomfortable in this building."* While some people might make fun of him for it, we believe that he deserves credit for having the guts to spend the night alone in a place like Farrar Elementary in the first place. For the record, we're not sure that either of us would be willing to do that!

John is hooked up to the brainwave scanner next, and the three men start out in the library, where the ghosts of children are said to play, and investigator Lisa Kovanda was sent flying through the air. He posits that using a spirit board can sometimes open a portal into our plane of being, either deliberately or unintentionally, depending upon the motivation of those who are using it. Tenney then goes one step further, and asks whether those spirit board participants could actually be *willing* some kind of entity into existence, creating it from scratch rather than simply allowing it to come through a portal.

This notion is not nearly as far-fetched as it may sound. We believe that we may have experienced a similar phenomenon at Malvern Manor, which is not too far from Farrar. The spirit of a young girl named Inez is said to haunt the Manor. For years, it was believed that she died of hanging up on the second floor, and that is the story that was told (in good faith) to countless groups of visiting paranormal investigators and curious para-tourists.

It was only when co-owner Josh Heard hired a private investigator to dig into the background of the building that it came to light that Inez did not die at Malvern Manor at all; in fact, she may never have even stepped foot inside the building during her lifetime. She actually died in a house several streets away. So how can it be that the spirit of a young girl has been seen and heard there, skipping along the second-floor hallway and answering to the name 'Inez' during spirit box sessions and on multiple EVPs?

It is our conjecture that the story of Inez dying at Malvern Manor became so entrenched in the folklore surrounding the place, a thought-form was somehow created, the by-product of years and years of cumulative belief in the story. Cultures around the world have their equivalent of the thought-form. To the Tibetan people, for example, it is known as the *tulpa*, and can be conjured at will if the desire to do so is strong enough.

Could the Principal have been brought into being in the same way? Or is this enigmatic shadow man coming and going via one of the multiple portals that are said to be found inside Farrar Elementary? We hoped to find the answers to this, and to many other questions, when we went there ourselves to investigate.

"I can imagine that a great deal of negative intent was poured into this very small, square space," David Rountree says, as the three men relocate to the principal's office. "And it's possible that it could be creating portal activity…"

Tenney is fascinated to see how his brain waves are responding to what he has been told about the most feared and dreaded room in the school, but before they go any further, Chad Lindberg is suddenly overcome by a feeling of intense negativity. The confines of the tiny office now seem far too hot to him, he says, the atmosphere oppressive.

David and John look forward to finding out if this will be reflected in Chad's vital signs, but as the electrical engineer tries to get a reading, the blood pressure cuff and heart monitor come back with an error. This is just the first of what will turn out to be a series of equipment failures that plague the *Ghost Stalkers* team at Farrar Elementary.

Leaving the principal's office, they head down to the boiler room, and after one last look around, it is time for them to kick off the first evening's investigation. To his credit, Chad steps up to the plate first. He enters the building alone, while Tenney watches events via a static camera and microphone that are set up directly facing the principal's office, while other cameras (without audio) are scattered throughout the building. John will also keep a careful eye on the front door, to make sure that nobody enters the school and disturbs Chad while he spends some quality time with the ghosts. All he has is a camera and a panic button which, if pressed, will set off an alarm in the RV outside and bring John running.

Chad starts out in the gymnasium and boiler room. John is unable to speak with him in there. In what we presume is an attempt to stir up some energies, Chad shoots some hoops, inviting whatever entities might be there to kick the ball back to him.

He is interrupted by a fairly loud tap, which makes him scream. On the audio commentary, he wonders whether this might be one of the spirit children playing, or possibly even the Principal 'gearing up for an attack.' (It is just as likely that this was simply the building's structure settling down and contracting after a hot day, and was a perfectly natural sound).

No further sounds follow, so Chad relocates to an upstairs classroom and breaks out a digital voice recorder. He begins asking the usual "what's your name"-type EVP questions, and receives quite the shock when a male voice replies with, *God damn it, Chad!*

As things seem to be heating up, he puts on an impromptu show for the spirit children in the auditorium. It's entertaining to watch him clowning around on the stage for an invisible audience, especially as it is being done in near-total darkness. It earns him another tap, which is just as likely to be random as paranormal, in our opinion.

Next, Chad hears what he thinks are footsteps, coming from somewhere outside in the hallway close to the Principal's office. If so, he would not be the first (or the last) to experience this particular phenomenon. Unfortunately, he doesn't go out into the hallway to investigate, and no further activity is documented during this first night. Chad is convinced that the noises he heard could be attributed to the child spirits which are said to haunt the auditorium.

The second night rolls around, and now it's John Tenney's turn to spend some time alone in the building. One interesting and striking point is the differing objectives that the two men have. While Chad is focused upon the presence of the children (he really doesn't like the idea that they may be left behind, years after their deaths) John is fascinated by the Principal, and seems determined to find out his identity. The reason we say that this is significant, is because the phenomena that the two men encounter inside Farrar Elementary seems to track with their area of primary focus. Chad wanted to find children, and believes that he did. John, on the other hand, went inside with the intention of finding the Principal, and would soon get exactly what he asked for…

John feels a presence shadowing him from the moment he steps inside the school, sticking right behind his back and following him wherever he goes. (Caretaker Will Conkel reports that he is feeling the exact same thing when the Principal is currently active).

He heads down to the boiler room, where Will encountered the Principal in the past. Pulling up a chair, he begins to run an EVP session, and feels a blast of cold air blow over him.

When he asks for a tap, he is given one in response. Once again, we must point out that this could just as easily be an entirely normal, everyday sound, such as a water pipe, but in that case, the timing would be extremely convenient.

Things get even colder — John hugs himself and says that it is 'freezing' — which is very atypical for the boiler room, even at night.

Based on the authors' experience, the room is not prone to cold drafts…not of the natural kind, at least. The odd temperature drop fluctuates, coming and going in waves. John's EMF meter dies, its battery drained; yet another unexplained equipment failure. John cannot shake the feeling of being followed and watched by unseen eyes, somewhat ironic when one considers the name of the show. The stalker is being stalked himself.

Unfortunately, the most compelling experience John has goes undocumented by the camera. While standing outside the principal's office, he catches sight of a shadow figure, seemingly materializing out of thin air.

He admits to being caught off-guard, and was therefore unable to photograph the figure. John is a talented sketch artist, however, and his drawing of the apparition shows a tall, spindly-legged figure with poorly-defined facial features that looks rather sad. John speculates on whether this might be the principal (though it lacks the glowing red eyes that Will reported the figure having) but his next comment is extremely though-provoking:

"It almost looked like two kids, standing on top of each other."

Considering the large number of accounts of children said to be haunting the third floor, does the possibility of two child spirit pranksters really sound all that far-fetched...?

Showing more backbone than many would be able to muster under the same circumstances, John goes after the shadow figure, but is unable to find it. He moves on to the library, in the hopes of encountering whatever it was that attacked visiting paranormal investigator Lisa Kovanda.

Just as he is settling down to conduct a recording session, Tenney is startled by something moving, caught in his peripheral vision — the shadow figure is back, this time standing in the doorway directly behind the camera that is set up there. It's beginning to look like a game of hide-and-go-seek (or possibly cat and mouse), with John feeling as if he is being hounded by the entity, which is also giving his cameras a very wide berth.

Seeking to confront the shadow figure on its own turf, John goes directly to the principal's office, which some have described as the epicenter of the haunting. Upon playing back an EVP session he has just recorded, Tenney is perplexed to find that nothing has been recorded — in the most literal sense of the word. All we hear is static. Even *his own voice* does not appear on the playback, indicating yet another inexplicable equipment failure inside the walls of the elementary school.

Despite our being seasoned paranormal investigators, this bizarre occurrence is something that neither of us have ever seen before. Suspecting that something in the vicinity of the principal's office is preventing the recorder from working properly, John heads one floor down, and runs a test session on the device while standing inside one of the classrooms. Once again, it fails to play back the sound of his voice.

Surely this is nothing more than a simple equipment malfunction? So one might think, and when John goes downstairs and stands next to the front doors (while still inside the building at this point) the recorder once again fails.

But the second he steps outside and tests it again, the device works perfectly, playing back his words loud and clear.

Heading back inside, John tests the recorder yet again. Yet again, it records nothing.

The conclusion is inescapable. Something inside the schoolhouse was interfering with his equipment. Perhaps the more important question is: why?

Discussing the matter with Chad the following day, John floats the possibility that a spirit portal could have been 'willed onto existence' in the vicinity of the principal's office. If true, that would explain the sudden appearance of the mysterious figure that he saw twice that night.

The *Ghost Stalkers* further theorize that the use of spirit boards, which has been carried out by multiple visitors to the school, might be to blame for the paranormal activity there. Tenney's opinion regarding the Principal is that he isn't actually a 'he' at all. The Principal is not even human, he says, describing it as "a powerful and unique being that dates back to archaic times," a sort of trickster/gatekeeper spirit that, in his words, "allowed energies to come back and forth between this world and the afterlife."

He goes further, adding that such gatekeepers could allow the spirits of former Farrar Elementary School pupils to return to the place where they were once so happy, running and playing in the hallways long after their death.

The gatekeeper, he says, also has a more somber purpose: preventing those of us who are still alive from getting definitive proof of there being an afterlife. To that end, this gatekeeper spirit will do whatever it has to do in order to keep people from figuring that out, up to and including acts of physical violence.

John had put forward quite a compelling argument, and as the end credits rolled, we knew one thing for sure...

...we really needed to hear it in his words.

They say that you should never meet your heroes, because they often turn out to have feet of clay. I was therefore just a little bit nervous about interviewing John E.L. Tenney for this book. John is a seasoned and highly-respected paranormal investigator of many years' standing. He has investigated and written about practically any aspect of the paranormal or the occult that you could possibly think of, and even one or two that might surprise you. Fortunately, he's also a really nice guy.

If you're not familiar with John's work, we encourage you to check out one of his in-person lectures, or alternatively, visit him online over at www.weirdlectures.com — or check out one of his books. If you're reading (and hopefully digging) this book, then the chances are that John is 'your kind of people,' as the saying goes.

John's brush with death at a relatively young age is what launched him on his path toward investigating the strange and the weird things of this world. As a 17-year-old, he was dead for more than two minutes. Before he was successfully resuscitated, John underwent an afterlife experience that was as intense as it was unpleasant.

Indeed, this was part of the premise of *Ghost Stalkers*. Both John and his co-star Chad Lindberg had been brought back not just from the brink of death, but from whatever it is that lies beyond it. They were, in many respects, the ideal duo to cross the threshold of Farrar Elementary and attempt to unlock its secrets.

"I love Farrar," John said after we had exchanged a few pleasantries. "It's one of those places that has a weird way of calling to you."

I told him that I knew exactly what he meant. Some haunted locations somehow exert the strangest sort of attraction, drawing you back in again and again. Although the buildings themselves may be old and, in some cases, crumbling, they are no less appealing for that. For me, locations such as Bodmin Jail in Cornwall, and the old Tooele Valley Hospital in Utah, meet this description perfectly. I have long since given up trying to fathom exactly *why* this happens; I just go with the flow.

I had spent a total of 72 hours at Farrar Elementary, give or take, and I already wanted to go back for more. Erik had been three times now, and was still up for a return trip whenever we got the chance to return.

First things first, however. I asked John how it was that he had come to be involved with Farrar. In another example of "it's a small world," John happens to be friends with Johnny Houser, caretaker of the infamous Villisca Ax

Murder House. Back in 2012, Johnny had asked him if he would be willing to come out to Iowa in order to attend a fundraising event, one that would raise a little money for the maintenance and upkeep of the school.

Never one to turn down the chance of investigating a haunting, John had been only too happy to oblige. The event took place the following year, 2013, and John spent a total of three days at the school. It was an eye-opening experience. After speaking to those who were gathered at Farrar that weekend to share their stories of the place, and hearing about their strange personal experiences first-hand, John soon found himself, in his own words, falling in love with the place. It is a love that persists to this day.

The sheer diversity of encounters impressed him. Eyewitnesses told John of experiencing everything from the sound of children running, giggling, and playing, to Johnny Houser getting slammed violently backward, his head striking one of the coat hooks. Clearly, whatever it was that was haunting Farrar Elementary defied easy explanation. It almost certainly could not be attributed to one single thing.

Within that same year, the green light had been given for filming to begin on *Ghost Stalkers*. The show needed locations in which to shoot, and John was passionate about making one of those locations Farrar. After all, what better opportunity could there be for him to gather more answers about this strange old school?

"It hadn't been on television yet, and wasn't really talked about," he pointed out.

John is absolutely right. At the time of writing (spring of 2019) the school has not yet featured on the shows *Ghost Hunters, Paranormal Lockdown, Kindred Spirits, Ghost Adventures,* or any of the other major ghost-hunting shows. Although fairly well-known among members of the paranormal interest community, as far as network TV is concerned, it remains a relatively undiscovered little gem. Why would that still be the case?

"Farrar is off the beaten path," John explains. "It's a 30 to 45-minute drive to the nearest hotel. It's one of those places that is kind of remote and secluded...and I think that's part of its allure."

He raises a good point. Much like the aforementioned Villisca Ax Murder House, Farrar Elementary isn't the kind of place at which one simply drops in if they're in the neighborhood... because there really isn't much of a neighborhood to drop into. Without insulting the local residents, which certainly is not my intent, this picturesque little place really is in the middle of nowhere. In order to get to Farrar, you really have to set out to *go to Farrar,* and you have to plan your travel accordingly.

Our conversation turned toward another aspect of the haunting that I found fascinating: that of the existence of portals. I was intrigued to hear John's thoughts on the subject, particularly as we had been told that either one or two of these doorways to another realm were said to exist at Farrar.

"When we pitched *Ghost Stalkers* to the network, there were a couple of underlying concepts that we used as a selling point," he began. "Firstly, Chad hadn't really investigated before, and I'd been doing it for years. That was one component. Secondly, there was this theory regarding portals.

"If there *are* ghosts, if there *are* these energies, and if they really can move between their reality and ours, then why are there only certain locations that are haunted? Not that there are necessarily portals, *per se,* but are there 'window areas,' places where the veil is thin. If they exist, these kinds of places would make it easier for them to walk back and forth between their reality and ours.

"When I explained it to the network in that way, they

really didn't understand it, so I ended up using the word 'portal' to make things easier to comprehend."

That started me wondering...*was* the veil between worlds truly thinner at Farrar than most other places? Perhaps that was why the school was so paranormally active. We had already heard the theory that the haunting was one hundred percent attributable to the land itself, and had nothing to do with the bricks and mortar of the school itself.

Saying the word 'portal' conjures up an image of some kind of revolving door (to our minds, at least) through which spirit entities can come and go as they please — a sort of 'rapid transit system for ghosts.' In light of John's comments, I was starting to rethink that. Perhaps the mechanism behind the haunting was more complex than it had seemed at first.

Building on that idea, my next questions surrounded the so-called 'big three' at Farrar — those entities which were most often said to haunt it. By this I meant the Principal, the Janitor, and the Librarian.

"Aside from the children, those *are* the most prominent entities there," John agreed. "One of the things that has always fascinated me most about Farrar was something that we never got to talk about on the show. You had this kind of 'trinity dynamic' happening, where you have these three major players. This has always interested me because I don't know whether I'm seeing three distinctly different individuals, or just three different aspects or facets of what is actually the same thing..."

This took me by surprise. Ever since my investigation of Farrar, I had proceeded on the assumption that we were dealing with a trio of ghosts, most likely the spirits of those who had once walked its hallways during their physical lifetimes. But what John was talking about here was something deeper: the possibility that the Principal, the Janitor, and the Librarian weren't the spirits of deceased human beings at all, but rather three separate faces of one single entity.

Wow. Mind blown.

"Think of it in these terms," John went on, warming to his theme. "You have the custodian or Janitor, the up-keeper; you have the disciplinarian, the Principal; and lastly, you have brain, which is the librarian. We see this occur a lot when we look at the world's religious, this idea of a trinity that gives a sense of balance. Think Father/Son/Holy Spirit, for example. The concept is very much the same.

I told John about the direct voice that I heard calling

down to me from the second floor, and said that I thought I may have encountered the Librarian. He agreed that this could indeed have been the case.

"You saw me have three experiences on *Ghost Stalkers*," Tenney went on. "One was in the children's library, the little room where the Ouija board session had taken place. I see a figure watching me from the doorframe, which makes me jump up off of the floor when I see it. To my mind, that was the Librarian aspect.

"Then, when I come through a doorway, I see the Principal, which freaks me out. I actually drew a picture of that, which they do show on *Ghost Stalkers*." Indeed, they do — it is a tall, lanky figure, dark and shadowy in appearance. "I actually gave Will and his wife a copy of that for their wedding.

"Finally, I feel like it was the custodian, or the Janitor as it's known, that was constantly turning my voice recorder off as I went back and forth from being inside to being outside."

The incident with the malfunctioning digital voice recorder was one of the more perplexing incidents from the show. I asked John if he still had it.

"I do. It's upstairs, in fact. I never used it again after

that night, though. It wasn't a USB-compatible recorder, and I wasn't able to transfer the file, so I wanted to keep that '*now it works, now it doesn't*' audio file from *Ghost Stalkers* on there for posterity. It'll probably stay on there forever."

John feels that during the course of his solo night at Farrar, he encountered all three of the major players, and that each of them made their presence known in a different way to the other two.

Going back to the drawing of what is believed to be the Principal, John reminded me that at first glance, the figure almost looks as if it has two heads.

"Now that I've looked at it for four years, I've come to realize that it doesn't really have two heads at all; now it looks to me like a tall man, standing behind a short child, with his hands on the child's shoulders."

"In the same way that you sometimes see when a parent and child pose for a portrait photograph," I suggested.

"Exactly."

"That would imply some degree of protectiveness, John, on the part of the larger figure."

"Yes, it would." Could the Principal, if that was indeed the entity that John had encountered and sketched from memory, have felt as if he (or it) had the need to in some way protect one of the child spirits from him? It may be that some of the fearsome acts which have been attributed to the Principal have all been nothing more than misguided attempts on the Principal's part to protect the young spirits of Farrar from what are perceived to be intruders — in other words, visiting paranormal investigators who have no business being there.

"The episode seemed to imply that the Principal was the one stalking you, John," I said. "Always standing in the shadows, just out of direct sight…but now you think that this was actually the Librarian?"

"Yes. Absolutely I do."

I asked him if he thought that the Principal got a bad rap, rather unfairly. That was certainly Will Conkel's perspective. Rather than being this dark and threatening entity, terrifying and full of malevolence as some have portrayed him, could the truth of the matter be that the Principal was doing nothing more than faithfully discharging the responsibilities of a protector… a guardian?

"I do," Tenney agreed. "Will and I have talked about that, in fact. Remember that we have all been children in school. We all have that innate, psychological wariness toward disciplinarian figures like that… the feeling that they have their eyes on us all the time, and they'll know if we do something wrong — and punish us for it. That gives us a feeling of unease, and the sense that somebody is trying to dominate us.

"Psychologically, I think that the Principal's presence manages to stir up a lot of deeply-embedded beliefs in all of us that have investigated at Farrar. You have to remember that these feelings were ingrained in us from a very early age."

John may just have hit the nail on the head when it comes to explaining why so many visitors to the school feel on edge as they walk through its classrooms and hallways. Could they be subconsciously perceiving the presence of an authority figure, standing in the shadows — one whose watchful eye was always upon them? The body could naturally react to that by generating feelings of foreboding and fear with no readily apparent cause.

We can't speak for you, dear reader, but the authors of this book are children of the 1970s and 1980s. The Principal of a school back in those days was a figure to be avoided, if at all possible, and certainly not somebody you wanted to get on the wrong side of. A visit to the Principal's office was usually something to be dreaded. It normally meant that you had done something wrong, and were about to be punished for it… sometimes physically. Corporal punishment may have been on its way out when we were in school, but for the first fifty years or so of Farrar Elementary's life, it would have been relatively common — and always painful.

"When I was a child, our principal used to walk the hallways and deliberately jingle the spare change in his pocket," John laughed. "That sound, of coins clinking against one another, would send waves of fear through every child that heard it."

It conjured up the image of a jailer walking the cell block, jangling his keys in front of the prisoners. Not a bad description of the way most of us felt about the principal back in the day!

The next thing we wanted to discuss was the identity of the Principal himself (or herself…or *it*self). It has often been presumed that the Principal is a male, but John's theory regarding the Principal, Janitor, and Librarian all being three aspects of the same being, had me pondering that now.

"What do you make of the theory that the Principal is none other than Will Conkel himself?" I asked.

"Think of it? *I came up with it!*" John chuckled.

It was an incredible idea, but one that made total sense

if you believe — as the majority of psychic mediums do — in the concept that spirit entities are not restricted to the same laws of space and time that we are. In this instance, the theory goes that when Will dies (hopefully many, many years from now) his spirit will return to the place he loves most in all the world — Farrar Elementary.

His love for the school quickly becomes very apparent to anybody who spends even a few minutes talking to him about it. As mentioned elsewhere in this book, he chose to get married there. It's his happy place. Why *wouldn't* he come back to Farrar in his own afterlife, assuming that he has any choice in the matter? Surely, I said to John, that makes sense?

"It makes *total* sense! That was one of the things I sat down and talked with Will about when I went to Farrar to perform his wedding. Think about it like this: He *is* very tall. He *loves* that place. He has been married in that place. He found the love of his life in that place. He has poured time and money and effort into that place, and above all else, *he takes care of that place.*

"So, is it possible that at some future time, after he is dead, is Will going back and still taking care of the place? It's something he's done his whole life now, so why would he stop after death?"

It would also go some way to explaining why Will feels as though he is constantly being watched by the Principal. Imagine, if you will, being granted the opportunity to revisit yourself in times gone by, walking around the place you were most fond of in the entire world. Talk about a trip down Memory Lane! We have to seriously consider the possibility that Will's invisible stalker is, in fact, none other than Will himself.

When it comes to the Janitor, however, John is far less certain about this particular spirit's identity. When coaxed, however, he is willing to venture an educated opinion.

"Think of the isolated little place that Farrar was, back in the day. The school was the focal point of the community. Everyone went to dances. Everyone had their weddings there. All the social events were held there. So much raw energy, memory, and emotion was poured into that place, that I can't tell you with any confidence if we're seeing the spirits of specific individuals, or some kind of... *amalgams* of collected memory.

"I've investigated Farrar four times now, and I've found that when you're separated — one group is up on the third floor, say, and someone else is down in the main hall

— it's practically unheard of to have multiple experiences going on simultaneously. *There is only ever one paranormal experience taking place at any given moment.* I found consistently that if you're running EVP sessions on the main floor and the third floor at the same time, only one of those groups is ever going to get a response."

I thought back to our own experiences at Farrar, and realized that he was one hundred percent right. When we had separated, Stephen had heard screaming, but neither Erik nor I had. Those strange events that we had experienced together, had only taken place when we were all gathered in the same place. It was almost as if whatever haunted the school was only capable of focusing its attention in one place at any given moment...

"The acoustics inside that place are pretty good," I said, thinking out loud. "Several times when my team split up, one of us heard a voice or a scream, but the other two heard nothing..."

"See, this is why I think it is one thing manifesting in several different ways. It seems to be able to take multiple different forms when it wants to. The spirit of Farrar itself, if that's what you want to call it, seems to pick a location and then go and watch that one thing. Then, once it's done there, it goes somewhere else and watches what's going on there. But it doesn't *ever* seem to be in two or three places at once."

"It doesn't ever multi-task?"

"Right. My instinct is that we're dealing with a single consciousness, one that changes form to suit its needs at any given moment."

If John Tenney was correct, then we had been working under a false premise all along. There weren't three individual spirits behind the Farrar haunting at all. There was just one, a chameleonic entity that only showed us what it wanted us to see.

That didn't necessarily mean that it was negative, or had nefarious purposes — if anything, I suspected that whether the Principal was the ghost of Will Conkel or the multi-faceted amalgam proposed by John Tenney, its primary interest was always going to be the protection of the school itself. Just as long as nobody threatened that, they would probably be safe within its walls...

... wouldn't they?

But then I recalled the frightening situation that had befallen Johnny Houser. Having one's head slammed backward into a coat peg could most definitely ruin your day

— not to mention paralyze you, if you were really unfortunate.

"We have to be careful of making assumptions," John said when I raised the issue with him. "We don't know how long those coat hooks have been there, or whether the Principal even knew that they *were* there. Did the Principal really mean to push him as hard as it did? Yet because of the situation, *we* make the assumption that there was malicious intent at work here. We can barely figure out the thoughts and motivations of our fellow human beings, let alone entities operating on another plane of existence!

"It's far too easy to misinterpret its behavior as something evil, something mad, something violent, but what we're really doing is making a judgment call based on incomplete information and our own biases."

I had to admit that he had a good point. Although many of those who have encountered the Principal have found it to be a frightening experience, there isn't a great deal about its behavior, when considered objectively, to suggest that it really means harm to anybody who respects the school.

In order to reinforce this point, John likes to share a story about a couple who approached him fifteen years ago, claiming that they had a demon in their house. John duly went to their house in order to conduct a preliminary survey. Plates were thrown in his presence. Doors were kicked open. He even sustained a bite before he left; leaving him in no doubt whatsoever that he was dealing with…

…not a genuine haunting, but two *extremely* badly-parented children. Before he left, John told the parents that he could not possibly investigate their house so long as the children were present and behaving like that. They were lashing out, he says, because they wanted attention. They weren't getting the attention and the care that they needed.

"When we deal with non-corporeal beings, it's a similar state of affairs," John went on. "We don't know how long they've been in that state, or how long they've been stuck in that location. Do we ever stop to think just how frustrating it might be for them to be in those locations? When they are finally able to muster up enough energy to touch your hair or push your chest, they may be doing so with a level of force unknown to themselves, accidentally plunging us down steps or pushing us into walls.

"We immediately assume that they're attacking us, when the reality of the situation could be that they might just not understand *how* to interact with us."

I have spoken about this same theme a number of times

in various books and presentations over the years. Imagine, for a moment, being newly deceased, cast out of the corporeal body that we spend decades getting used to, and suddenly finding yourself as a disembodied spirit.

Everything is new to you. How do you touch things? How do you make yourself seen, heard, or felt? After an unknown amount of trial and error, the sheer frustration that must build up would be immense.

If the only way in which you can make your presence known is to lash out, then you are almost certainly going to do just that.

It is entirely possible that this explains much of the aggressive behavior that is attributed to 'demons' and 'dark entities' in a large number of hauntings.

"Think of it in these terms," John continued. "You and I can go and sit in a library and read a book for two hours, no problem whatsoever. We'd think nothing of it. After all, we have the knowledge that we can get up and walk out whenever we want. We don't even think twice about it.

"But now imagine that you're in that same library, but this time you're *stuck...* not for two hours, but for two *years...* or even for two *decades*, or longer. That's a whole different story. You're practically guaranteed to become angry, upset, or just plain lonely."

"It could quite literally drive you insane," I said, taking John's point to its logical conclusion.

"Sure," he agreed. I took a moment to let the implication of that sink in. Could it be that the Principal, as I was beginning to think of all three of the primary entities which had been reported at Farrar, be insane?

Was it angry, and out of its collective mind with loneliness? If so, that would go a long way toward explaining some of the more alarming phenomena which had been reported at the school, including Johnny Houser's experience with what appeared to be a physical attack. Changing tack, I asked John to share his thoughts about the ghostly children that so many visitors had heard at Farrar. Did he think that they were intelligent or residual? "At Farrar, I think you're getting a mix," he opined. "Because of the very deep schoolhouse memories, and the energies which build up around them, people who have passed away like to go back and visit. I suspect that's why it's hard to get an accurate track on which children are always there. Some of them like to go back and visit, walk the halls, and then they leave. The next day, two more show up.

"Remember that when you're dealing with *real*

children, physical children, it's hard to get them to talk in the first place. There's stranger danger, and all that. Plus, there's this feeling for them of being in the school when they're not supposed to be. Based on this coming-and-going, I suspect that it would be virtually impossible for us to track exactly *who* was in that school at any given time, even if you could get them to speak and then tie their identity in to that of a former pupil.

"During the 1920s when the school first opened, this was probably the one place of stability and security that many of those children had in their lives. That stability came in the form of their friends, teacher, and classroom. Those were all constants in an uncertain world. Who wouldn't want to revisit those days, if they were given the chance to do so?"

The man had a point. If I had the opportunity, I would happily walk the hallways of my first school. It would evoke feelings of great happiness and nostalgia.

I asked John for his thoughts on there being nature spirits involved with the haunting. Will Conkel and Coyote Chris Sutton certainly believe that they are a fundamental aspect of the paranormal activity that takes place there. Tenney, for his part, is less sure.

"I do somewhat agree, but only to the extent that no

matter where you go in North America, you are, to some degree, always on, or close to, an Indian burial ground. I don't think that it's a very large component of the haunting overall."

In terms of potential energy sources that could be used to fuel the paranormal activity, we have the owners, Jim and Nancy, who live on-site for much of the year round. They generally restrict themselves to their private quarters on the main level, however, and they have taken strong measures to put psychic protection in place that covers their home from intrusion. The community surrounding the school is rather small, barely hitting the double-digits. But now we have to account for the constant influx of paranormal investigators and para-tourists that flock to Farrar all year, but most especially when the weather is good during the summer months.

Every single one of them arrives with their own set of expectations and beliefs, not to mention a desire to experience something paranormal themselves, in the flesh, so to speak. That is a great deal of potential energy for the spirits of Farrar to use in order to manifest, and use it they most assuredly do.

"There's a kind of energetic field that surrounds us

when we start to think about this other world, the afterlife," John agrees. "Remember, too, that there is a cemetery directly across the street from Farrar. It may not be large, but cemeteries are places where there is often an outpouring of grief, which brings its own kind of energy along with it. How do these two types of energy — the sadness and grieving associated with the graveyard, and the joy and happiness that suffused the school — how do they both connect and interact with one another? What is the end result of that interaction?

"If there are spirits in that cemetery, do they find themselves attracted to the happier light of the school, and perhaps get pulled in? In other words, it's possible that they might be drawn to the school like moths to a flame."

"So, it's acting like a lighthouse or a beacon of some kind?" I asked.

John is in agreement.

"Sure. That place feels to me like it is just *full* of spirits," he says, before adding that most of them seem to come back to visit, rather than remaining earthbound as permanent residents. "A lot of 'ghost hunters' are in it for the scare factor, rather than to carry out genuine research. Their aim is to get spooked. They go in there, muscling up and acting tough, just as they have seen on TV.

"They're screaming, they're shouting, they're banging on doors — just generally being disrespectful…and I'll tell you what, I was a custodian in a high school for a while. If kids see an adult acting crazy in a school, then those kids will go crazy too. Guaranteed."

"They'll take their cue from the adult?" I interjected. "Yes, exactly. And it's my belief that this is why Farrar has its caretakers… the Librarian, the Janitor, and the Principal. They have watched people go in there, screaming and shouting, bringing in all of their own problematic psychology, and as a direct response, the school has manifested the beings that it needs to keep itself safe."

When he put it like that, it made absolute sense to me. Rather than ghosts in the traditional sense of the term — in other words, the discarnate spirits of the dead, hanging around and interacting with the living — John Tenney was proposing that the energies which suffused Farrar Elementary and its surrounding environs had coalesced into thought-forms, energy-beings that were created in order to fulfill a very specific purpose. Paranormal entities as a defense mechanism. The very idea of it is brilliant.

Many cultures from all around the world have their own

variant of the thought-form concept. As stated earlier, the example that I most commonly like to cite is that of the *tulpa*, which originates in Tibet.

More recently, the so-called 'Philip Experiment,' that was conducted in Canada, demonstrated with some degree of success that it was possible for human beings to generate their very own thought form and imbue it with some degree of intelligence and purpose.

Why could the same thing not have happened at Farrar?

"We — the living — are the virus in this case, and Farrar is protecting itself," John said. "The ghosts are antibodies. It's a good idea not to piss them off."

As our interview came to a close, I asked John whether there was any aspect of the Farrar haunting that he felt we had not covered or anything that he would like the readers of this book to know.

His answer, quite honestly, surprised me.

"Despite its reputation, there are a few things that happened at Farrar that were extremely *funny*. We didn't have the time to put a lot of that stuff into the *Ghost Stalkers* episode."

"Like what?"

John was down in the basement, conducting an EVP

session. The session had lasted for about thirty minutes so far, and he had gotten precisely zero responses.

"Okay," he had said, getting to his feet. "I'm leaving for the day."

Playing the recording back, he heard nothing but dead air.

"Man," John grumbled as he made his way out of the building. *"This fuckin' place…"*

He hadn't actually realized that he had still been recording. It had been an oversight; John believed that he had switched the recorder off, when in fact it had still been running. It was only when he played back this particular section of the file that he realized he had caught his only EVP of the day.

After hearing himself grumble, "This fuckin' place…" John could clearly and distinctly hear a voice reply, *Fuck you, Tenney!*

Upon hearing the unexpected EVP, John instantly burst out laughing. Farrar had given him absolutely *nothing*, right up until the very last moment, and when he had walked out of the building, shaking his head in disgust… there it was, as plain as day.

A Class-A EVP.

Not just that, but one that pointedly mimicked his own obscenity, throwing it back in his face.

Another memorable experience was part of the shoot for *Ghost Stalkers,* but never made it into the finished episode when it aired on TV. John was directly outside the principal's office, speaking both to the locked-off video camera and a hand-held digital voice recorder.

"Can you tell me what you see?" he had asked, a fairly innocuous question. "*How* do you see me? Can you tell me what you see?"

No response.

"Do you see in colors?"

A sound came from somewhere off to John's side, as though something small had just hit the floor. When he looked to see what it was, John was somewhat bemused to spy a yellow crayon lying on the floor next to him. It most definitely had not been there before, and he could only assume that it had been apported in answer to his question — a happy, kind manifestation that he was only too happy to witness.

"Don't forget that Farrar can be *silly*, too. It is a school, after all."

"Kids played there, all day long," I added.

"Right. That's why I was so keen to get Chad up on that stage and have him start clowning around when we did *Ghost Stalkers,* I wanted him to play the flute and do a play. That's exactly what that stage is *for.*"

And it seemed to work. Which led me to my final question. I pointed out to John that he and Chad seemed to have been given exactly what they wanted by the school. John had voiced an interest in encountering the Principal and learning more about him, whereas Chad was all about the ghost children that were said to haunt the place. In each instance, Farrar seemed to give them exactly what they had asked for.

To my mind, at least, this seemed far more than mere coincidence.

"The spirits are picking up on our intentions," John explained. "Yes, ghosts don't have ear canals to physically hear our voices, but they do have the ability to read our minds, and I think that's how Farrar and certain other locations react to us — by reading our minds and reacting accordingly.

"Across all cultures, the most common form of spirit interaction, done by the most people, is *prayer.* They close their eyes and speak silently in their mind. They expect, believe, and *know* that their thoughts will be heard… so why wouldn't that also hold true at a haunted location?"

Why not, indeed?

Chapter Eight

E. E. Bensen:
Interview with Steven Tracy

I had a chance to speak with Steven Tracy, founder of Iowa Paranormal, for about an hour regarding his experiences at the Farrar school. His first visit was in 2010, and he reported that nothing particularly paranormal had occurred. The school was quiet; although he was quick to point out that he wasn't there for very long either.

Conversely, in July of 2011 on a subsequent visit, Steven told me that his team had experienced what was, and still remains to be, one of the most active nights of paranormal investigation that he has ever experienced. He also indicated that the third floor of the Farrar school where the auditorium is located is one of the most haunted places that he's ever been to. Given my own shocking experience on the third floor, I certainly cannot dispute this claim myself.

In previous years, the auditorium was actually divided into four separate rooms. There is still evidence of this today in the form of long strips of missing carpet on the floor. I have never seen the area in that state, therefore I can only try and relay what Steven described to me in terms of layout. I hope it is at least somewhat accurate as a result of the retelling. Apparently, there was a pathway or hallway running along the back wall that provided access to a small set of stairs leading up to the main stage, and also afforded access to the other rooms within the area. The stairs to the stage still remain to this day, and I've walked them myself more than once.

While standing near those stairs, Steven and a team member witnessed what he described as a human figure standing at the top of the stairs that seemed to react to their presence, before politely walking into the nearby wall and disappearing. That particular wall happens to be an exterior one, meaning that the space just on the other side of it is actually around thirty feet off the ground.

Steven described the figure as being between five and six feet tall, and that it looked wavy, much like the mirage heat shimmer effect that one sees while driving on long stretches of road in the summer heat. He was quite excited to share this story, and I was equally thrilled to hear it. After all, as a paranormal researcher, it really doesn't get much better in terms of the possible experiences one can have. What Steven saw is precisely what we're looking for, and surely what keeps us wanting for more in the long run. I can only imagine how utterly startled and excited his team must have been.

Later that night, while sitting on the stairs to the stage area, the team heard a very clear female voice talking in one of the nearby rooms. As usual, upon inspection, they found no evidence of anyone being in the area, and could not arrive at a sufficient explanation.

As he relayed this story to me, my thoughts immediately drifted to our own recent experience with the friendly audible voice that responded to us from the second floor. Perhaps we heard the same woman nearly eight years later. If so, I always have to wonder what "life" is like for her. Why is she there? How does she see the world? What exactly is going on in her dimension or space? Is she really a "she?" These are of course, unanswerable questions, but fascinating nonetheless. Cases like this are made even stranger given the woman we heard, clearly knew *we* were there, but we could not see her. Paranormal investigation never ceases to be strange, that is one thing I can say for sure.

Another occurrence that Steven reported experiencing on that same night was the clear and distinct sound of footsteps walking around the third-floor hallway. I had actually heard something very similar during our visits to Farrar as well. He was quick to point out that the steps were very obvious, and not simply a distant sound that could be mistaken for anything else. This is another thing that always baffles me. In my ever-growing list of paranormal experiences, I have heard clear footsteps, and even loud bangs on a door. How is it that something with no apparent mass can produce such sounds? I think some would be quick to say that perhaps it is just residual audible phenomena that has been somehow recorded in the environment and played back, which is fair enough, except that I've witnessed the banging happen on command before. Again, this is very strange.

On yet another visit in May of 2012, while investigating the third floor, Steven reported seeing a pair of white misty human legs appear in the doorway to the principal's office. Before disappearing from sight, these legs walked to the right and into the desk located in the room. Again, the similarity to one of my own experiences in the school was uncanny. I witnessed the same thing in the auditorium on a prior visit, and what I saw would have been very close in proximity, just a few feet from where Steven had his experience. I will also note that I have seen a very similar phenomenon in multiple haunted locations in the past, most notably and recently, at Malvern Manor in Malvern, Iowa. There, I was treated to a fleeting glimpse of ghostly legs wandering around the nursing home wing on the first floor on multiple occasions and visits.

Later that same night, Steven's team asked for an unseen presence to slam a locker door, and they were immediately treated with an extremely loud sound that was consistent with their request.

I have noticed that the perception of the haunting at Farrar varies quite a bit among experiencers. Some believe the haunting to be very negative, while others feel that it is relatively innocuous.

I asked Steven what he thought, and he indicated to me that while he has a hard time being anywhere alone in the building, he hasn't been attacked or harmed in any way. Still, he did say that equipment setup is an activity best left for the daylight hours. I certainly can't pass any judgement on this, as I've felt that way in numerous locations over the years, most notably at the Washoe Club in Virginia City, Nevada. That place scares the hell out of me.

As for Farrar, my own experience is somewhat different. I have no problem walking around the place alone during the daytime, but I'll have to agree with Steven that after dark is a different story.

He and I agreed that the place turns notably more ominous in the dark, and that there is a constant sense of being watched, or not being alone. This is actually one of my favorite things about Farrar, as strange as that may sound to a non-investigator. Often times the school will not let you forget where you are, and I love that about it.

Steven prefaced his last story with a statement that I've heard numerous times in my travels, "This might sound crazy..." I don't believe that he had read either of my books; otherwise he'd have known that I specialize in sharing stories that sound like that to most people. Simply put, nothing sounds crazy to me anymore after the experiences I've had. The things that I have been fortunate enough to witness in my own paranormal investigations have forced me to be completely open to just about any story. I've been left with no choice.

A few months prior to this writing, Steven was involved in hosting a public ghost hunting event at the school. He was in the boiler room on the lower floor and relayed an experience that he clearly had a difficult time articulating, and I fully understand why.

At one point, he asked a question to one of the event participants, and suddenly noticed that he had gotten no answer. In fact, he suddenly had a distinct feeling that he was the only person in the entire building. He described it as feeling like he had somehow dipped into another time and place, or dimension, or that he had experienced a time loss of sorts. Immediately snapping out of it, and falling down physically in the process, he was perplexed by the overwhelming and alarming feeling that he had just been alone in the building.

While I know that he was hesitant to share this particular experience due to the high strangeness of it, I'm really glad he did. Anyone who takes paranormal research seriously, and has had a wide array of experiences, will surely find interest in this one. I've had my own run in with what I think was a time slip during a local investigation here in Colorado, although mine resulted in audio evidence and lacked the physicality of his. As is always the case, paranormal research only gets weirder and murkier the deeper you immerse yourself in it.

I enjoyed talking to Steven about his Farrar experiences. During our conversation it became clear to me that he is one of the "tribe" as well. A seemingly honest and humble researcher merely searching for answers with a level head. I love meeting people like that, because in a field as divisive as this one can be, we need all the good folks that we can get. Before hanging up the phone, Steven was sure to remind me again that Farrar is his favorite place to investigate. That is certainly saying a lot given the places he has been, and it is well deserved in my opinion

Chapter Nine
Richard Estep:
Interview with Seth Alne

Our next interviewee was to be film-maker Seth Alne. Seth specializes in making paranormal documentary movies, and had just released one that focused upon Farrar Elementary.

Having spent forty-five nights in the building made him something of an expert on the place, and we were looking forward to gaining his unique perspective on the haunting.

Back in 2010, Seth was working on a documentary project titled *Haunted Iowa*. When Nancy and Jim offered him the opportunity to pay a visit to their haunted schoolhouse, he jumped at it.

Farrar Elementary was less well-known than it is today. He had heard nothing about the place being haunted via the usual paranormal grapevine, but found the idea of a haunted school to be an intriguing one. The first thing to do was a little background research. Browsing the Internet, Seth could find a few references to ghostly activity supposedly taking place at Farrar, but it sounded like minor-league stuff… lockers slamming, doors opening by themselves, and a few other anecdotal reports.

There was nothing to indicate that the place was particularly active, in the paranormal sense of the word.

Still, it was somewhere fresh and relatively un-investigated, and so Seth put together his basic investigational kit, a couple of movie cameras, and drove on out there to see for himself.

He had arranged to spend a single night in the school, more as a preliminary test of the activity levels than anything else.

If things turned out to be flat, he reasoned, he would still have a few minutes' worth of footage to add to *Haunted Iowa*.

Accompanying Seth were his brother, and three other paranormal investigators, along with Johnny Houser. Once they arrived and got a brief tour of the place, Seth and his crew got down to business. The first thing that needed doing was for somebody to run DVR cabling up to the third floor.

As he reached the third floor, Seth realized that something about that floor felt, for lack of a better word, *off.*

It was the same feeling he'd gotten in high school when he was walking around the corridors without a hall pass, hoping not to get caught; a feeling of 'I really have no business being up here.'

Both he and the female investigator that had accompanied him to the third floor shared the same feeling, and found themselves constantly looking over their shoulders towards the principal's office, where that sensation seemed to be at its strongest.

"*Something* was watching us," he says, looking back on it almost a decade later. "Something we couldn't see…"

With the cameras all hooked up and rolling, it was time for the investigation to begin. The team split up into smaller groups and went their separate ways. Seth chose to go back up to the third floor with Johnny Houser.

Heading over to the principal's office, Johnny made a flippant remark about the Principal of the school. Even before they could play back the audio recording afterward, the sound of inane giggling was clearly heard. It was the kind of snorting laughter that school children would make when somebody told a particularly crude or stupid joke. The fact that both investigators had heard the giggling with their own ears made the phenomenon more of a direct voice than an EVP, and based upon the timing of it — coming right on the heels of Johnny's comment — the evidence suggested that it was an intelligent response, rather than something residual.

Making their way to the opposite end of the hallway, Johnny revealed that he was getting the strong impression that a child — most likely, a girl — had been placed in some sort of great jeopardy in that part of the building at some point in time. He 'saw' flashes of a big, shadowy figure menacing her, though none of the details were clear.

No sooner had Johnny said that, than Seth felt a surge of energy rush up the length of his spine, and for no apparent reason that he could see, he suddenly burst into tears. He was suddenly overcome with a wave of intense grief, one that was immensely strong and had come right out of nowhere.

One minute, Seth and Johnny were strolling through the classrooms; the next, Seth was on the ground, sobbing uncontrollably.

This was only the beginning of what would turn out to be a very paranormally active night at Farrar Elementary. One of the stranger experiences occurred in the break room, which isn't known as one of the more haunted parts of the school. Seth's team member was shocked to see the face of a wizened old woman come flying out of the wall towards him, only to disappear into thin air just as quickly as it had materialized.

During a ghost box session, a number of unpleasant messages began to come through, including one which claimed to have been the Principal himself.

The voice gave a name, which Seth was unable to verify as having been an actual principal of Farrar Elementary. It is also possible that this was the voice of a negative entity, one attempting to pass itself off as a former principal of the school.

A female member of Seth's team experienced some unwelcome physical contact throughout the night, feeling hands touching her in a number of places, all of which she must have found more than a little disturbing.

Later that evening, the female investigator was up on the third floor, along with Seth's brother Jesse, and witnessed the astonishing sight of a shadow figure form behind Jesse.

The shadow figure had, she related later, a look of 'pure evil' upon its face, and seemed to be staring intently at Jesse's neck. At the very same time, Jesse suffered a significant panic attack — one so severe that he was practically unable to breathe.

They wasted no time in getting him out of the building. Once outside, a flashlight revealed that a series of angry red marks could be seen upon his neck, almost as if an invisible pair of hands had attempted to strangle him.

This violent episode set the tone for many of the visits that Seth's group would make to Farrar over the course of the next couple of years. He recalls there having been a significant bout of darker, angry interactions with the spirits of the school, particularly where female investigators were concerned.

At first, Seth and his colleagues attributed this negative activity to the Principal; after all, this particular entity has often been portrayed in a negative light, catching the blame for most of the more frightening incidents that have been reported at the school. Yet as time went on, Seth would begin to see things a little differently.

It is now Seth's belief that the Janitor is actually the spirit that is responsible for physically touching visitors. He noticed that almost every time somebody was about to get touched, the faint sound of jingling could be heard — as if the Janitor was shaking a set of keys.

This is, of course, difficult to tell for sure. As with so many aspects of the Farrar Elementary haunting, it is difficult to accurately determine which spirit entities are responsible for which phenomena — let alone figure out their motives and patterns of behavior. We will make some educated guesses on that particular subject in this book, but it is fair to say that when it comes to the specific nature of the spirits of Farrar, a great deal still remains to be learned.

As time went on, the interactions that Seth and his fellow investigators had with the spirits seemed to grow angrier and more aggressive. When the team had positioned themselves downstairs, for example, they would hear loud banging noises coming from the floors above them. It sounded very much like somebody was repeatedly punching one of the lockers. Whenever anybody went up to check, the sound abruptly stopped.

"I think that the touching was done by the Janitor, and the violent stuff was the Principal," Seth says, before going on to talk about the time when his investigators encountered the apparition of what they believe to be the Principal upstairs on the third floor. "He was wearing a suit and tie. His face was a mask of pure rage. I can tell you that he's definitely very mad about *something…*"

"What do you think he's mad about?" I asked.

"About us being there, and digging around at the school. When I gave tours at Farrar, there were a number of times when I was all alone in the building, waiting for the tour group to arrive. That's when I hear him pacing, up there on the third, these big, heavy footsteps thudding on the floor. He'd go back and forth, back and forth. Then the lockers would start slamming.

"When we went up to the principal's office, the closet door would start opening and shutting all by itself. The doorknob would twist and turn. It was like he was determined to scare us out of there.

"Then things were taken to the next level. People started to get taken over."

"Taken over," I asked, "As in...*possessed?*"

"Right. My brother, Jesse, was taken over, for one. So were others. Johnny Houser was one of them. He sat down in the Principal's office, closed his eyes for a little bit, and then all of a sudden began talking about how he'd choked somebody. He said that he hadn't meant to choke them so hard. Then, just like that, he snapped right on out of it, and said, 'Dude, I don't know what just happened!'"

The image of a confident and experienced paranormal researcher such as Johnny Houser being taken over, even temporarily, by an unknown influence is a disturbing one. This is a man who deals with the very worst psychic phenomena that the Villisca Ax Murder House can throw at him on a daily basis, and keeps coming back for more. He is very strong-willed and isn't easily intimidated, which implies that whatever it was that overcame him for that brief period of time, had to have been immensely powerful.

They were accompanied by a former stuntman and musician who is well-known for his role on a prominent network TV show. This gentleman, who shall remain nameless, is a big guy, powerfully built, and a reassuring presence to have at your side in a dark and haunted place. After Johnny's apparent take-over, the stuntman walked into the Principal's office to find him still sitting in the chair.

"All I wanted to do just now was hit you," Johnny said, eyeing the powerhouse of a man who was standing in front of him. If he had actually done so, it would no doubt have turned out badly for Johnny.

A female visitor said that she felt 'supreme anger' toward the stuntman, and wanted to push him down the stairs. Considering the fact that this man is said to be one of the nicest men you could wish to meet (and I would add that Johnny Houser most certainly is too) this seems like a very strange reaction for two people to have toward him.

It may well be that the Principal, or one of the other resident spirits of Farrar, felt threatened by his formidable presence, and were somehow influencing Johnny and the woman, trying to goad them into a physical confrontation.

Then Jesse got in on things, squaring up to the stuntman and getting right in his face. At 6'5" tall, most of it pure muscle, he towered over Jesse, but that didn't stop Seth's brother from fixing him with a stare that was meaner than a hungry rattlesnake.

Johnny, Jesse, and the female visitor were all acting way out of character, showing a very uncharacteristic and totally unwarranted level of aggression toward an affable man who was just minding his own business.

What — or perhaps *who* — was to blame for this? Seth has his own theory for that. He holds Farrar Elementary accountable for it.

"That place is just crazy, man," he laughs. And if the testimonies of the hundreds of paranormal investigators and casual visitors who have visited the school over the past ten years are to be believed, then he is absolutely right. "You've got to understand that the school has changed a lot since I was there regularly, a few years ago. It *feels* different now."

"Different in what way?"

"I think that somebody brought something in, probably through the boiler room. That room used to feel totally dead; now, it's *very* active. That being said, the Principal seems to be there less often. He was always a very physical spirit, pushing people around and shoving them whenever he got the chance."

Seth went on to tell me about the time he had a 300lb-plus cage fighter at one of his ghost hunting events. This particular gentleman was a complete skeptic, and therefore had no hesitation in accepting Seth's suggestion to go up to the principal's office and 'push him a little bit.' He had been in there for no more than a couple of minutes when something unseen side-checked him into the wall, knocking the breath out of him.

Nor was Seth to be left out. Perhaps unwisely, he attempted to goad the Principal himself, once again choosing to do so on the Principal's home turf — his office. Suddenly, from out of nowhere, he felt a burning sensation in his face. As his team-mates hurried to take pictures, an angry red mark started to develop, spreading rapidly across the surface of his face. There had been no obvious force involved, no slap or impact.

There has been a great deal of speculation surrounding both the appearance and the identity of the Principal (including some conjecture regarding whether 'he' is even human at all). The common narrative currently holds that the Principal is a tall shadow figure, sometimes seen to have glowing red eyes; yet Seth offers a different take. He notes that whenever he *and* his colleagues have seen this particular apparition (or his shadow), the Principal does not appear to be a shadow figure all the time. Instead, he appears as the ghost of an angry-looking man wearing semi-formal attire, usually a button-down shirt beneath a tailored suit. His hair takes the form of a widow's peak.

Crucially, when Seth and his fellow investigators have seen him, the figure isn't particularly tall, and certainly isn't Will Conkel. This is an excellent example of the confusion that surrounds the identities of the prime movers among the spirits of Farrar.

Pinning down exactly which shadow figure or apparition could be the Principal, Janitor, Librarian, or someone/ some*thing* else, is an almost impossible task.

One thing which cannot be argued is that the third floor, which contains the office of the principal, is the most paranormally active floor. It is not at all unusual for otherwise fit and healthy investigators to find themselves inexplicably out of breath when going from the second floor to the third, after climbing just one story higher. The atmosphere up on the third floor can also change on the spur of the moment, thickening and becoming oppressive for no apparent reason.

Seth points out something that Stephen, Erik, and I discovered for ourselves — the fact that one's eyes rarely adjust on that floor. It is as if the darkness somehow takes on a life of its own, and tiny pinpoints of multicolored lights streak across the walls when least expected. This bizarre, almost sentient form of darkness seems to almost *absorb* the light, even when there is a full moon riding high in the sky outside.

Remembering the female voice that the three of us had heard calling out a response to me from the second floor, I enquire whether Seth had encountered this phantom lady for himself. While he had not had a direct voice experience similar to ours, he does reveal that on his first night at Farrar, a young woman's voice had come through on the spirit box up there.

Rather than shedding any light on the nature of the haunting, the words that she spoke only served to deepen the mystery.

The baby…I'm saving it.

Which naturally begs the questions: whose baby, and what are you saving it *from?*

Over the space of the next couple of years, the woman's voice became a semi-regular speaker over the spirit box. She claimed to have loved somebody (possibly the Principal), always speaking in the past tense. Her voice often reduced those who listened to it to tears, overcoming them with a terrible sadness that none of the witnesses could explain.

I asked Seth for his thoughts regarding John Tenney's theory that the Principal might be none other than Will Conkel himself. After considering it for a moment, Seth ultimately rejects the notion out of hand. He points out that Will is 'the gentlest giant you'll ever meet,' whereas the Principal has something of a reputation for behaving combatively… especially if provoked. While that may be true, I counter with the perspective that, if the observations of Seth and his team are correct, then the Principal and the big, tall shadow figure are most likely not the same entity. After all, one of them is a fairly average-sized male apparition with clearly-defined features and hair, dressed sharply in a suit and shirt, whereas the other is a significantly taller shadow figure, sometimes seen with glowing red eyes, sometimes without. Although there had been multiple accounts of people provoking the Principal and receiving a violent response, that didn't necessarily mean that those responses were coming directly *from* the Principal. In addition to that, there was still the issue of the Janitor to be addressed.

"See, this is what attracts me to Farrar so much," Seth enthuses. "Once you walk through those doors, you just never know what you're gonna get…"

That leads me neatly toward the question I had been asking every single person that I interviewed for this book: why, in his opinion, was Farrar Elementary so haunted?

"Back in 2010 or so, there was a lot of debate among members of the paranormal interest community about whether Farrar was even haunted *at all*," he begins, adding that a number of people had simply dismissed it all as being nothing more than one big hoax. "I learned differently, from my own experience. When I started looking into the school's past, I talked to multiple former students who said that back in its heyday, Farrar Elementary wasn't necessarily a nice place to be."

When I asked him for concrete examples, he told me that several of them had claimed that some (though by no means all) of the teachers ruled with an iron fist, and were not beyond applying corporal punishment to the children when they felt that the situation warranted it. This went on, he said, as recently as the 1980s. While this may indeed be true, physical punishment alone doesn't account for the paranormal activity at Farrar, in my view. If that were the case, then every single school that pre-dates the 1970s or 1980s ought to be similarly haunted, as would every military school and barracks. The answer has to be more complex than that.

"This place generated fear," Seth continues, "and based on my experiences with the Villisca Ax Murder House, I know that fear can physically manifest."

There have also been somewhat nebulous allegations concerning black magic being practiced in the vicinity of the school, though I was unable to find any evidence of such happenings taking place.

"Looking back on the three years that you gave tours at Farrar, and all the time you spent investigating and filming there, what are the most compelling things you experienced?"

Seth pauses to think about this for a minute, before telling me that the most remarkable thing took place in the gymnasium at a public event. He and the guests were spending the entire weekend at Farrar, sleeping in the gym overnight. He woke up in the early hours of the morning to the sight of a young boy, dressed entirely in white, who was walking among the prostrate forms that were slumbering on the floor. The boy was staring up at the ceiling, yet still somehow managed to avoid making contact with any of the sleepers.

His mouth agape, Seth turned to wake up one of his neighbors. When he turned back, the boy had vanished into thin air. He recalls the experience vividly to this day, describing the boy as being dressed in white jeans and a white t-shirt. A skeptic might say that Seth simply dreamed it all, but he counters that argument by saying that he immediately related the experience to a fellow investigator, who remembers him being fully alert and excited at the time.

Assuming that this wasn't a dream or a hallucination, as Seth insists, then a full-bodied apparition is an impressive thing indeed. Yet Seth has encountered much more at Farrar than that. After telling me about hearing the sound of drawers and doors rattling in the empty building, he mentioned the time when he happened to be whistling to himself... only to have the whistle reciprocated from upstairs, somewhere on the deserted third floor. I immediately recognized the strong parallel between that and our own experience with the female voice, which also replied to us from above.

At Farrar Elementary, there are few coincidences.

There was the case of Seth's colleague, who bravely elected to spend a few hours alone in the school one night. It was the dead of winter, and not a soul was about. Even Jim and Nancy, the owners, were away, enjoying warmer climes.

The man was setting up a camera tripod on the infamous third floor, when suddenly he felt a sharp pain in his leg — something akin to a pinch. Rolling up his pant leg, he saw three distinct scratches on the flesh beneath, deep enough to have drawn blood.

After having been in the school for just four hours, he had had enough. The scratch was too much for him to handle, so he hurriedly packed up and left.

"I also want to talk a little about the boiler room," Seth goes on. "When I first came to the school, nothing much happened down there, paranormally speaking. It was pretty much flat. Now, things are really starting to ramp up down there, and I'm starting to buy into the portal theory a little more.

"I'm telling you, Richard, something has *changed* down there, and whatever it is, it's not good."

I'm intrigued by that, because during our own time down in the boiler room, the most alarming thing we had encountered was a bull snake. I ask Seth to expand on this a little more.

"The last time I was down there, I was absolutely *terrified*," he says. "The atmosphere was completely different than before, so much so that I was pronouncing the name of Jesus in order to protect myself. I was almost prepared to go out on a Zak Bagans-style limb and say that there might be a demon down there! It felt *that* dark to me, and do you know what? It wasn't there before. Somehow, a door has been opened in the school that has let whatever that entity is come into the building, and it isn't restricted to the boiler room either."

"You're saying that this dark entity can also manifest throughout the rest of the school?" I ask.

"Yes, exactly. I talked to Will just the other day, and he told me that he could see dark figures crawling around the ceiling in one of the second-floor classrooms. He wanted to know where that had come from, because that sort of manifestation had never been seen at Farrar before. And I had to tell him that I had no idea, but I do think that something is opening up there, and that something is getting worse."

I'm not sure that I like where this is heading, but I ask the next logical question anyway.

"If that really is the case, Seth, do you think that we're contributing to that — to making things worse — by continuing to carry out paranormal investigations there?" "Absolutely I do," he replies, without hesitation. "You're feeding it... fueling it. Who knows how this is all going to turn out?"

Who knows, indeed?

Chapter Ten

Richard Estep:
Interview with Meegan Campbell Rios

My interview with film-maker Seth Alne had given me
plenty of food for thought. He had tipped me off to the fact
that his colleague, Meegan Campbell Rios, seemed to have
gotten a lot of personal attention from one of the entities at
Farrar, and so interviewing her about her experiences was
the logical next step.

Meegan has had a life-long fascination with the
paranormal, which stems from some strange experiences she
had as a little girl when her family was living in a fairly old
house.

As a high-schooler, she began watching the multitude
of ghost-hunting shows that were springing up on TV, and it
dawned on her that there was no reason at all why she
couldn't become a paranormal investigator herself. She
saved up to buy a digital audio recorder (still one of the most

effective tools in the paranormal investigator's kit!) and set out to find some answers for herself.

She started out in cemeteries, and then moved on to the homes of friends who claimed to be having odd experiences.

None of these experiments yielded much in the way of results, but Meegan was taking her first steps on the road to bigger things. It was while attending college that she first met Seth Alne, who, along with his brother Jesse, shared her fascination with all things ghostly. After joining their team, she began to learn more and more about the tools and techniques of paranormal investigation.

Meegan first went to Farrar in 2010, and what she experienced there was, in her own words, "an absolute game-changer for me." She has never looked at the paranormal in the same way since.

"It was the first time that I ever had a deep, personal connection with a haunting," she tells me, before adding, "And *not* in a positive way, either. There is definitely something unnerving and quite dark there."

"Which spirit do you mean?" I ask, pointing out that there are several.

"The Principal… at least, that's what it refers to itself as in our audio recordings."

It's interesting to note that Meegan speaks about the Principal as an 'it,' rather than a 'he.' The implication is that this is a non-human entity or force, rather than the spirit of a deceased individual.

"I got a very weird vibe from the second I first went into that building," she continues. "For whatever reason, something there stuck to me. It may have been a name thing, because on one of our audio recordings, we got the name 'Megan,' which is pretty close to mine."

As we have already seen, visitors to Farrar have experienced all kinds of phenomena, running the entire gamut from seeing shadow figures and apparitions, to hearing voices and being touched. Meegan's experiences were primarily of a physical nature, and she classifies them as being some of the most intense encounters of her entire career as a paranormal investigator.

She claims to have been choked by an unseen force; felt herself being pushed (and almost fell down the stairs as a consequence); and had her legs grabbed, leaving vicious red marks on the flesh in the shape of fingers. This is quite the laundry list of things for a relatively new investigator to cope with, and it was not lost on any of those present that all of these interactions came in the form of an attack. Meegan found herself deeply shaken by these encounters, but refused to allow them to scare her away from Farrar.

As if all of that wasn't enough, she then went on to see the only full-bodied apparition of her entire life... the Principal. When Meegan reveals this to me, I press her for details. What did he look like, exactly? Most sightings of what is believed to be the Principal describe a tall shadow figure, sometimes with glowing red eyes, sometimes not; what Meegan saw, however, was something entirely different.

"He looked like an actual person. I could see his eye color, skin tone, hair color, everything." As she talks about the man that she had seen, I notice that her description of him tallies almost exactly with that given to me by Seth. "I've always approached the paranormal with an open mind, but also try to maintain a degree of healthy skepticism. In the past, whenever an eyewitness told me that they had seen an apparition that looked as solid as you or I do, I always thought that their mind might have been playing tricks on them.

"All that changed instantly when I saw this man for myself. The feeling, the experience, is almost indescribable. He was so *clear*, I can still see the expression on his face."

Meegan may claim that the situation was indescribable, but I ask her to describe it anyway.

The entire team of investigators was present in the building at the time. Meegan was up on the third floor, standing next to another investigator in the hallway. Her fellow investigator suddenly seemed to be overcome by something, growing flushed and starting to feel dizzy for no apparent reason.

Just as any good paranormal investigator would, she immediately started to film her colleague, in the hope of capturing something in the way of evidence.

Almost immediately, the freshly-charged camera battery drained down to practically nothing, tipping her off that something was using it as a convenient source of free energy.

Looking back up from her attempt to troubleshoot the camera, Meegan was astonished to see the form of a dark shadow figure standing directly behind her fellow investigator. She is adamant that this was not *his* shadow, but rather something separate and independent. Her colleague seemed blissfully unaware of his shadowy companion.

"I don't want to freak you out," she began, "but—"

That's when she saw that the mysterious figure had changed, going from a dark and featureless human-shaped shadow into the fully-realized, three-dimensional apparition of a middle-aged male. The man was simply standing there, looming over her partner's right shoulder, and was glaring down at him with what Meegan describes as 'an extremely nasty scowl' on his face.

The implication of this was clear: Whoever this entity was, he (or it) did not like the fact that the investigators were inside the school.

"Right away I panicked and began to freak out," Meegan laughs. "It felt very much to me as if the apparition was aware of our presence and didn't want us there. He never looked directly at me or made eye contact — his attention was focused completely on the other investigator. It would subsequently be discovered that he had somehow developed bright red hand prints on the skin of his neck.

Uncharacteristically, Meegan jumped backward and screamed at her partner that there was somebody right behind him.

Both Meegan and Seth believe that she may have been the recipient of so much spiritual attention because she is a female, and therefore found herself targeted by some kind of opportunistic negative entity within Farrar. Multiple spirit box sessions conducted there would give up the same name: that of a male, which the authors of this book have decided to keep confidential, in deference to that person's living relatives.

This particular entity made a number of unsavory comments and disturbing claims during those sessions — comments of a particularly salacious nature with regard to females. When Meegan and her colleagues tried to look into some of those claims, they were unable to find any evidence at all to substantiate them; she is quick to point out that this particular entity may never have worked at Farrar, or even have lived in the town. In many cases, spirit entities can attach themselves to paranormal investigators at one location, and then accompany them to another place, taking up residence there.

"I've also experienced a lot of playful energy at Farrar," Meegan goes on. "The laughter of children; tiny footsteps; and toys being moved. These are all things that I've run into there. So, there's definitely a lighter side to the haunting, in addition to the darker stuff."

Why is Farrar Elementary haunted, and haunted to such a great degree? As with the other interviewees, she isn't one hundred percent sure.

"We did unearth a legend that a young child is supposed to have drowned in a ditch quite close to the school," she muses, before adding that once again, she hasn't seen any concrete evidence to support that particular story. "The cemetery may be contributing to it, but I still don't know why Farrar is so active. Whether it's the building, the location, the people who walked its hallways… I just don't know."

I round off the interview by asking Meegan about her thoughts on the identity of the Principal. Could it really be the spirit of Will Conkel, returning after his future death to protect his beloved school?

After all, Meegan has set eyes on this particular spirit entity directly, and can still see his face.

"The man I saw was younger than Will is now," she responds, after thinking about it for a moment. Thanks to the magic of social media, however, Meegan was able to check out some photographs of a younger Will. "He *does* kind of resemble the apparition I saw. Maybe there is something to that theory after all…"

Our time now at an end, I thank her for sharing her thoughts and experiences regarding this enigmatic old school.

"Farrar is an *amazing* location," she says, wrapping things up. "I have not had a single visit to that place which has disappointed me. The things I have experienced there had deep impacts on my life. Farrar is, hands down, my favorite haunted location to visit. It always leaves me wanting more…"

We know exactly how she feels.

Chapter Eleven

Richard Estep:
Interview with Lisa Kovander

I had seen Lisa Kovander being interviewed on the Farrar episode of *Ghost Stalkers*. From the way that the episode portrayed her experience there, it appeared that she had undergone a violent and terrifying encounter with the spirits of the school, and I was looking forward to hearing Lisa's version of events in her own words.

Her first brush with the paranormal happened at the age of 21, when she lived in a house that was haunted, she says, "and not in a good way." Lisa would frequently wake up to find a male apparition standing in front of her. He had a frightening visage, mainly due to the appearance of his face being very severely burned.

She had the distinct impression that this spirit wanted her out of what he saw as being *his* house. Lisa got out of bed most mornings to find all of the drawers and cupboard doors standing open, knowing full well that they had all been closed the night before.

Dishes would be stacked in the middle of the living room floor. Sheets and blankets would be torn off the bed. Nobody could blame her for finally taking the hint and moving out as soon as the lease expired.

How did she first become acquainted with Farrar Elementary? Originally, it was used as a training ground for members of her paranormal research team. It wasn't a long drive, and the price was very affordable.

"I have *never* had a time when I went to Farrar that it wasn't paranormally active in some way, shape, or form," she says. She knew the place was truly, genuinely haunted when she felt a pair of invisible hands touch her in the center of her back. It felt to her as if her back was ice cold, and two distinct handprints were visible when Lisa's colleagues looked underneath her shirt.

From then on, her team recorded multiple EVPs. They witnessed a desk physically moving, right in front of their eyes. This was in the early days, before Farrar Elementary had gained a widespread reputation as a haunted location.

During one of the investigations, a colleague of Lisa's was conducting a spirit box session outside the principal's office. He was, she admitted, being rather provocative, which can sometimes be a very unwise tactic to employ. Little wonder that a voice came out of the speaker and declared: *Stop it...or I'll kill you.*

Our conversation soon turned toward the incident with the spirit board that had gained Lisa no small measure of notoriety, thanks to its dramatization on *Ghost Stalkers*.

"I gained this nickname of being 'the entity summoner,'" she laughs. "John Tenney had fought for my section of the show to be toned down a little, but if you watch the episode today, that's not exactly the path they went down."

Lisa is referring to the fact that her use of a spirit board in one of the classrooms, coupled with an aggressive physical interaction that interrupted the session, is used to imply that she opened some kind of doorway inside the school library that would allow dark entities to manifest there. The spirit board didn't belong to Lisa. It had been left at Farrar by a former visitor. Lisa says that she had gotten permission from Nancy to make use of it, while simultaneously recording the session on video and also placing sensors all about her. Nancy granted her permission to do so as well.

"One minute, I'm working at the board," Lisa recalls. "The next, I feel this pair of hands shove me. And I do mean *shove*. They slammed me a good six feet across the room."

"You actually felt hands?" I ask, wanting to clarify the incident as much as possible. "Physical hands, as opposed to some kind of energy field?"

"Actual hands," she confirms.

"And who do you think it was that pushed you?"

"The Principal. Our Ouija Board session had started out with playful responses. The girls and I were talking with what sounded like a playful child. The spirit of one girl, who is said to have special needs, is said to spend a lot of time in the library, and we thought that's who was communicating with us."

Maybe, I think to myself. *But it's also possible that whatever you made contact with was only pretending to be a child...*

"Then suddenly, everything changed," Lisa goes on. "The messages started getting more intense. 'GET OUT,' that kind of thing. Somebody else was talking to us... and that's when I got slammed."

It is interesting to note that, while the digital voice recorders didn't pick up any EVPs during the spirit board session in the library, what they *did* record was an audible *whoosh,* immediately before Lisa was pushed across the room. To this day, she does not have an explanation for the sound.

"Do you think that the Principal was trying to protect the spirit of the young girl?" I ask. "Or was there some other motive at work?"

"I got the impression that he didn't want the kid or kids to talk to us," Lisa responds after thinking about it for a moment. "At the same time, I also felt that he might have been trying to push me away from something... something bad. I think it was definitely a case of, 'I don't want to talk to you on this board, so we're done.' One of my fellow sitters made a big mistake when the planchette went to goodbye: She said, 'No, there's no goodbye. I still have questions.' That's when the Principal decided to get our attention in another way. She should never have said that. He really didn't want those kids talking to us. We were disrupting his classroom."

That strikes a chord with me. "You were a troublemaker in his eyes, then. So, he disciplined you..." It's a sobering thought, but I remind myself that there are still a number of possible alternative explanations to consider.

Once the session was over and Lisa had recovered her equilibrium, she elected to destroy the board. This involved breaking it into multiple pieces, salting the fragments, dousing them in holy water, and then burying them in the earth, alongside the planchette, which was first broken in half.

All of this took place in another state (Nebraska), so its connection with Farrar should have been well and truly broken.

To Lisa's credit, she didn't pack up her equipment and high-tail it out of there, as many people would have done. Not only did she stay, but after a fifteen-minute break, she doubled down and returned to the library once more, to see whether her attacker was still hanging around.

While nothing came of this next session, in an upstairs classroom, one of Lisa's colleagues suffered something akin to a panic attack when she became convinced that some invisible force was trying to choke her.

It would be quite some time before Lisa would cross the threshold of the elementary school again.

During the TV shoot for *Ghost Stalkers,* Lisa returned to Farrar in order to film her interview. She was told that various members of the crew would be walking around, carrying out tasks and setting up for future shots; Lisa should just ignore them.

Once her interview had been shot, she asked exactly who it was that had been messing around on the stairs behind her. Nobody had been on that staircase during the filming, and yet Lisa's friend had seen what she described as a pair of child-size girl's shoes and white socks at the top of the staircase throughout the interview (she had been unable to see any further up because the ceiling blocked her view). Once the cameras stopped rolling, the feet had disappeared.

Lisa tells me that she feels the episode of *Ghost Stalkers* portrays her and her team-mates as having gone into the school with a spirit board and then opened up a number of doorways that were best left closed. In reality, she points out, somebody else had brought the board with them beforehand, and they had been the ones to use it inside the school. It is also possible that many other visitors had done the same thing.

Once the board was destroyed and buried, did this have any effect on the paranormal activity inside the school? "Nancy told me that there was a whole different vibe there," Lisa says. "Much more positive than it was when the board was still there."

It has always been my opinion that a spirit board is a tool just like any other, and that employing one is no more dangerous than using a spirit box, an Ovilus, the Human Pendulum, or any other technique that is intended to make contact with discarnate entities. This is purely my opinion, of course, and there are many people out there who believe that such boards should never be used, due to the potential for opening up a door that may never be closed again.

"My problem with the board is that you have more than one person opening themselves up to allow a spirit to manipulate them," Lisa says. "That makes me nervous. Allowing those spirits to work through you, to use *your* hands, puts you in a position where you're letting an unseen entity *inside* you, and it may not really be little Sally-Sue, no matter who she claims she is."

That also makes perfect sense to me, and while I have personally never had a negative interaction while using a spirit board over the years, I have spoken with many individuals that have. Considering what happened to Lisa in the library at Farrar Elementary, I would be greatly surprised if she ever wanted to put her hands on one again.

Out of respect for Jim and Nancy's wishes, we had not used a talking board during our investigation at Farrar. With the benefit of having spoken to Lisa about her own experience there, I can't say I'm sorry that we did not.

What of the different spirits who are said to haunt the school? Lisa believes that the Janitor is most often found downstairs; the Principal tends to remain upstairs (though not exclusively); and both the Librarian and the children can usually be found on the middle and upper floors.

"When Jim and Nancy first bought the building, the spirits thought that they were going to tear it down. Now, I think they realize that's not going to happen. Those spirits are trying to protect the building. It's their home, after all."

This makes complete sense to me. I had heard others — most notably John Tenney — broach the theory that the ghosts at Farrar are doing nothing more than defending their home from what they might very well see as a constant stream of intruders. At the end of the day, it's as good an explanation as any for some of the more violent and frightening phenomena that have been documented there.

Next, we turn back to the possibility of the so-called child spirits not actually being children at all, but rather, something much more sinister. Lisa agrees that it is often extremely difficult for a paranormal investigator to tell what kind of entity they are dealing with, particularly when communication is based purely upon a spirit Board or a spirit box.

We are very easily fooled sometimes, and like all people, thanks to our in-built biases, are prone to hearing exactly what we want to hear.

"The spirit that pushed me may have realized what this 'child' actually was," Lisa points out. "In fact, it may have been trying to help me, firstly by telling me to get out, and secondly by physically pushing me toward the exit."

"So, it might have been the Principal, or one of the other resident spirits, trying to protect you from something evil," I suggest.

"Quite possibly," she concedes. "With a place like Farrar, you just never can tell…"

Finally, comes the key question: Why is Farrar Elementary haunted?

"Like so many other people, I've done the research, and there's no obvious reason," Lisa says. "There isn't the murder, the tragedy, the brutality that you see in so many other badly haunted locations. My team and I walked across the street to the cemetery. It's quiet and peaceful. We didn't sense any spirits hanging around there, and our equipment didn't pick anything up.

"I can see why the Principal, the Janitor, and the Librarian would still be there — they're the protectors. But why would the kids be there? I've heard them talking and laughing on EVPs, so I know that they *are* there... but I still haven't figured out why."

All I can do is nod. Lisa is most definitely not alone in that regard, and I leave our interview having gained some real insight regarding her experience with the talking board, but absolutely none the wiser as to the reason behind it all. As the good folks at TAPS would say, "On to the next..."

Chapter Twelve

E. E. Bensen:
Interview with Craig Nehring

Craig Nehring is the founder of the Fox Valley Ghost Hunters, and has visited the Farrar school numerous times. He is also an author, and has published a few books on the paranormal that can be found on Amazon. I was able to chat with Craig for about 45 minutes, during which time he shared several impressive stories regarding the old schoolhouse.

During the team's first visit, Craig reported that a female investigator had felt the sensation of a child hugging her. She was completely freaked out and refused to leave the break room for the duration of the night. She left the group permanently the next day. In my experiences as an investigator, I've seen this occur a couple of times. Often people are excited and curious to have an experience, but I don't think all of them actually think it will ever happen.

When it does, sometimes it is just too much to handle.

Craig went on to say that two other investigators would experience this same hugging phenomenon on future investigations.

Perhaps the most intriguing report that Craig offered was that of an investigator accidentally leaving a large Maglite flashlight sitting on the auditorium stage overnight.

The next morning, they returned and headed upstairs to retrieve it, only to find that it was missing entirely. Positive that the light had been left there, the team set about reviewing a video camera that had been left running in the room, facing the stage.

The flashlight was clearly visible for a long period of time, and then as Craig described it, the thing just simply vanished. It was there one second, and literally gone the next.

In paranormal terms, apportation is the transference of an object from one place to another. In some cases, it has been blamed for the permanent disappearance of an item. This may well be the first time I've ever met anyone claiming to have caught this on camera however, and I'm very intrigued by the report. Given my own strange experiences in the school, I cannot cast much skepticism on the subject.

A few years ago, shortly after the passing of my stepfather, my mother reported that she had cooked dinner for herself and set the dining room table with a plate and silverware as she always does. Upon returning to the table a short time later with food in hand, she noticed that the silverware was gone. As anyone would, she stood there for a moment staring at the empty spot next to the plate, then simply decided that she must have been mistaken and returned to kitchen to retrieve more. Upon returning to the dining room, the silverware was sitting there plain as day next to the plate. I love that story, as it is just the sort of thing that he would have done.

The mechanics behind the disappearance of objects is baffling, but nonetheless, reports abound. I have heard many stories in my life of people losing and looking for specific objects, only to eventually find them in plain sight in a spot that they had checked numerous times previously. I've actually had this happen to me more than 20 years ago. In my case, it was my car keys. I ransacked my apartment looking for them over a period of about ten minutes, only to turn around and find them sitting politely and prominently on the table where I always left them. I had checked that table several times, including looking behind, and under it.

This happened prior to my deep dive into the paranormal field, so I did what most people do, and just locked it away as something strange, but probably explainable. I reasoned that I must have been distracted and missed them somehow. Yeah, right! Humans will tell themselves anything to sleep better at night.

As for the flashlight at Farrar, it was never recovered. For the following few months, other paranormal teams would go on to report that they had witnessed from the outside someone walking around what should have been a vacant school, with none other than a flashlight. Craig was quick to point out that this particular report is something that he cannot substantiate as he did not witness it, so advised me to take it with a grain of salt. I pass it on to you, Dear Reader, with the same cautionary disclaimer.

Craig went on to report that he was sleeping on an air mattress in the break room, when something unseen punched it, and woke him up. Other investigators reported having the covers pulled off of them in the early hours of the morning while sleeping on another mattress in the same room.

I've actually had this mattress punching thing happen to me once as well, and I had never made the correlation until literally now as I write this. It must have happened around the same time as the missing car key incident; because I know it was the same apartment. I only lived in that apartment for a year total. The story goes about the same, I was completely asleep, and awoke suddenly in the middle of the night due to what I can only describe as a firm punch or hit on the mattress. I was single at the time and living alone, so I can't attribute it to any other person. I recall waking up very groggily, looking around the room, then just assuming that I had twitched or something and jostled myself awake. This had never happened before, or since, for that matter, therefore I must also dismiss my handy explanation at the time. I just rolled over and went back to sleep.

Craig went on to rapid fire various experiences that have taken place over the years which I'll simply summarize here as we didn't talk about them in too much depth due to time constraints.

While sleeping in the auditorium, the team heard footsteps running in from the hallway, and captured what appear to be two apparitions on video moving rapidly. An investigator reported something running up to and also *onto* his air mattress in the auditorium. Again, while in the auditorium, investigators heard lockers on the lower floors slamming open and shut for several minutes straight. Most were afraid to go down to the bathroom for quite a while.

Around this time, they also reported hearing something rummaging through Craig's bag as he slept. Another investigator left the team after hearing footsteps in the auditorium one night, and reporting that a large black shadow was hovering over her and holding her down. The list goes on and on…

Last year, Craig had the opportunity to be a part of the Amazon show, *The Paranormal Journey*. Due to a video filming glitch, unfortunately the episode will never see the light of day; however, he *did* have an impressive experience to share. The host of the show had setup a tent outside the building to use as a base camp, and was running a white noise device. Unlike the various flavors of 'geo-boxes' or 'spirit boxes' that you can see on most paranormal shows these days, this particular one had nothing fed into it in the way of phonetics, speech recordings, or radio signals of any sort.

After running for some time, the white noise device began playing what sounded like a basketball game in progress, complete with the sound of a ball bouncing and sneakers squeaking on the floor. I will remind you that the box was *outside* of the school at this point. As would be expected, the team brought the device into the school and headed straight for the gymnasium.

Although the physical environment was quiet, the phantom basketball game persisted through the speaker. Cleverly, Craig and team decided to place geophone devices on the free throw lines. These are essentially vibration detectors. They observed multiple instances of the geophones alarming in conjunction with the sound of a ball bouncing, coming from the white noise device. Craig was quick to point out that the gym floor is very solid, likely having a concrete substructure. I can attest to this myself as I've been in that gym many times now. The floor definitely has no hollowness, or 'give,' to it.

I asked Craig why he thinks Farrar is so haunted, and also whether he thinks it is a negative haunting in general. He explained that perhaps the school was a happy place for many people, and that somehow after death, souls of those who previously spent their formative years there, continue to roam the building and play together today. He was quick to point out that some of the activity there is surely residual in nature, and nothing but a playback of some kind. However, there is a decidedly intelligent aspect as well, and I can attest to that myself. We agreed that it would be quite odd to have presumably gone to the school, and then lived a full life, only to end up opting to return to the school in death. The paranormal field is full of conundrums like these. I offered a theory that perhaps in death, the soul is multi-threaded somehow. Maybe we can do many things simultaneously, and enjoy all of them equally. Perhaps the intelligent spirits haunting the Farrar school are but strands of a whole, spread out across many places and times, and involved in a myriad of things.

Craig went on to say that he doesn't feel the haunting at the school is negative in general. He did relay a quick story of an investigator that had broken group protocol, and apparently wandered off and began provoking the spirits in an attempt to elicit a response. That person was rewarded with scratches on his body.

As the guys pointed out in the *Ghost Stalkers* episode, if you provoke anything in the place, it is willing and able to fight back. The way I see it, this is a reflection of human nature in general, and also a reasonable response from whatever it may be that roams Farrar today. Craig also indicated that once an investigator sneezed during an investigation, and they were rewarded with an EVP recording that stated, "Bless you." I found this extremely amusing, because during our investigation of the Villisca Ax Murder House described in this book, I sneezed during an EVP session, and we picked up exactly the same gentle response. We have it on video.

The last thing Craig shared with me was that he likes to play a friendly game of Marco Polo in the school. He has yelled "Marco!" on several occasions, and a few times was fortunate to receive either an audible disembodied voice or an EVP recording that replied "Polo!" in response. During a more recent visit while the team was running a ghost box device, they were thrilled to hear a lone voice push through the white noise, presumably from somewhere beyond our reality. It said only one word: *Marco!*

Chapter Thirteen
Richard Estep:
Interview with Coyote Chris Sutton

I knew even before sitting down to interview him that Coyote Chris Sutton was quite the interesting cat.

In the past, he and I had chatted briefly in passing, but didn't know one another all that well.

I had been told that he had some fascinating insights into the haunting of Farrar Elementary, particularly given his status as a practicing shaman, and I was really looking forward to picking his brain on the subject.

Chris first became aware of the school thanks to its appearance on *Ghost Stalkers*.

Although he didn't know exactly why, he felt himself being drawn to the place, and instinctively knew that it would somehow be a part of his future. After reaching out to Jim and Nancy Oliver, he arranged to participate in a public event being held at the school later that year.

"One thing about Farrar," he explains, "is that everybody always focuses on the *inside*. The school, the structure itself. People forget about the grounds that surround it. The event itself was pretty cool. We got some paranormal activity, though it wasn't exactly off the scale, it was a pretty decent amount.

"But through this whole thing, I keep getting drawn outside, to that big old grandmother oak tree out there. I was still trying to figure out why, of all the haunted places I'd ever visited, I felt so strongly drawn to Farrar, and I was convinced that oak tree was a big part of it..."

All night long, Chris had been inside the school, but his mind kept showing him images from outside. He knew that was where he was really meant to be, and once his obligation to the event had concluded, he made a bee-line straight for the main entrance doors.

Stepping out onto the grass, Chris approached the tree and stood in front of it. Tentatively, he reached out and placed both hands on the trunk, feeling the rough bark against the skin of his palms.

In his shamanic practice, Chris is very sensitive toward the energies of the Earth itself. The moment his hands made contact with the tree, he felt a sudden influx of energy flowing from it. There was a moment of spiritual communion between man and tree that formed the connection Chris had been so fervently seeking.

"I'd make contact with David Rountree through Facebook," Chris continues, "and ask him about the tree. It's his belief that many of the energies there, center around the oak tree. That's exactly what I thought too, and I knew that I wanted to go back and explore it more deeply."

To that end, Chris set up another event at the school. Dan Klaes (owner of New York's haunted Hinsdale House) came along as a guest.

Chris resolved to spend a significant part of the investigation outside, focusing on the grounds in general and the tree in particular.

They also arranged to bring in a psychic medium, who immediately began picking up on sensory impressions that appeared to be Native American in nature.

All of the participants were singing around the base of the tree. Some were drumming. Chris could feel the energy levels rising within the tree itself. As related in an earlier chapter of the book, this is the night on which Will Conkel felt the spirit of the oak talking directly to him, in what proved to be a truly moving personal spiritual experience.

A GeoPort device was running at the periphery of the circle. Chris claims that voices from the box were speaking both his and Will's names, and also asking for the story of the Farrar spirits to be told. When the night was over, many of the participants left feeling deeply moved by what they had experienced in front of the school. Some were actually quite shaken up. The following evening, the focus was going to be primarily indoors. Once again, the GeoPort began speaking Chris's name, and those of other people who were there.

Chris believes that the spirits of Farrar were once again making their voices heard.

After the structured activities had been completed, the attendees were offered free time, allowed to roam wherever they wanted to for the rest of the night.

Standing quietly and watching from the sidelines, Chris was struck by the fact that so many of them seemed to wander off into the darkness, only to come right back to the big old tree, seemingly as mesmerized by it as he and Will were. It was almost as if the oak exerted a magnetic-like pull upon them, drawing them right on back to it no matter how far away they went. As with most of the other people that I interviewed for the book, Chris cannot say why Farrar

Elementary is haunted.

"I just don't get it," he says, shaking his head. "Nothing major happened there that I can tell, or find out from its history. But my best educated guess is that most people are looking for an explanation in the wrong place. Everybody looks at the school, and they're all ignoring the grounds.

"It's almost as if they built this school on top of holy grounds, for want of a better term. There are great Earth energies there, and Farrar Elementary sits right on top of them, and they're energizing the structure itself. The spirits that come to Farrar don't necessarily *belong* there. They're just feeding off the energy. I've seen this happen in other places."

I ask Chris about the theory that tough disciplinary conditions at Farrar were the cause of the haunting, at least partially.

He believes emphatically that this is not the case. "I never got that feeling from the energies I picked up on there," he says. "I don't think this haunting is rooted in something of that nature."

What of the spirits that haunt the school?

"There are a number of negative spirits at Farrar," Chris confirms, "But then again, there are children present too. I think that's mostly because they liked it there."

I go on to ask Chris his thoughts about the theory of there being a trifecta of spirits — the so-called 'big three' — at Farrar. Has he ever encountered any of them in person?

"I have felt the Principal, but he did not engage me. It was up in his office on the third floor. I didn't find his energy to be combative or antagonistic, but it most definitely was *not* friendly, I can tell you that."

"'Not friendly' doesn't necessarily mean evil, or malevolent, does it?" I point out. "This could just be a guy who wants what he sees as intruders to get out of his space."

"Exactly," Chris agrees. "Sometimes the spirits are just grumpy. Others are territorial. For me, when I walked into his office, I went in with a respectful attitude. I didn't feel the need to spiritually protect any of the other people present, or to get into it with him. He wasn't attacking anybody, as I have seen some other shadow people do."

"What about the Janitor?"

"He mostly stays downstairs. The first time I went to Farrar, the Janitor was down in the boiler room. I walked in, and he immediately climbed high up into the pipes, right up there near the ceiling. The Janitor sat up there and he wouldn't come down. Once again, it wasn't a pleasant feeling to be near him, but I didn't sense anything truly nasty about him… it was more the sense that he just didn't want to be bothered with our company. A 'just leave me alone' kind of thing."

"Do you see them as two distinct entities — the Janitor and the Principal?" I want to know.

"I just don't know," Chris shakes his head. "The first time I was there, I encountered the Janitor but not the Principal. The second time, it was vice versa — I ran into the Principal, but not the Janitor. So, it's impossible to say for sure."

"What about the Librarian?"

Chris tells me about his first visit to Farrar. He and some fellow investigators went up to the library, in the hopes of interacting with some of the child spirits that are believed to be active in that particular part of the school. Elizabeth [Saint, of TV's *Ghosts of Shepherdstown*] took a children's book down from one of the shelves and began to read aloud from it.

All of those present could sense the atmosphere inside the library becoming increasingly warm and wholesome, a sensation which became stronger the more she read.

"It was as if something in that room was very pleased

with Elizabeth for reading from that book," he reflects. Whether this was emanating from the spirits of children or coming from the Librarian herself, it is impossible to say. Either explanation makes sense when put in the context of the bigger picture.

I tell Chris about my own encounter with what I believe to be the spirit of the Librarian, as I called out goodnight when we were leaving the building.

"That sounds like her," he chuckles. "I have often felt a very positive female energy in that part of the building, especially when people are quiet and acting respectfully."

"There's a real sense of *balance* at Farrar," I muse. "There's both a light side and a dark side to the haunting."

"Absolutely. If you go in there and you taunt, if you're provoking, then you're going to have a bad time." Chris goes on to relate the story of a visitor who went into the school with a belligerent, completely dismissive attitude, calling out that the whole thing was nothing more than a 'big crock of shit.' Just as he was getting ready to wrap up for the evening, the person in question collapsed onto the floor, rendered semi-unconscious by some sort of unseen intervention. His companions ultimately had to carry him outside the school, sitting with him outside while he regained his composure once more.

Chris is quick to point out that he heard this story from two different sources, both of them being people he considers to be extremely reliable.

Sometimes, karma can be very quick.

I'm fascinated to learn what Chris makes of the theory that there are multiple spirit portals at Farrar.

"Having come across vortexes like that in a number of cases, feeling the energy and actually seeing them swirl, as Dave Rountree attempted to demonstrate with the fog experiment on *Ghost Stalkers*… I do think it's possible," Chris says. "I didn't feel a portal outside the principal's office, as some people have said, but then again, there are other people — like Will, for example — who know the place much better than I do. I didn't sense portals anywhere there, though I *did* feel something very odd right at the back of the stage in the auditorium. It's difficult to say for sure.

"My feeling is that the Native American spirits tend to stay outside the school, and won't go inside. You're looking at something entirely different to explain the paranormal activity going on within those four walls…"

As our interview draws to a close, we come to the conclusion that the haunting at Farrar seems to be an aggregation of the Native American spirits and Earth energies outside the school, along with the Principal, Janitor, and Librarian inside the school, supplemented by the spirits of what may or may not be children in the vicinity of the library.

Chris points out that it is also possibly a mix of residual and intelligent paranormal activity, with some spirits being resident there, and others being in-transit, dropping in and out according to their own timeline and personal agenda.

We are both in agreement that the haunting of Farrar Elementary is one of the most complex and challenging cases we have ever encountered during our respective careers spent investigating the paranormal, defying easy explanation.

Small wonder, then, that we both find the place so very compelling.

Chapter Fourteen
Richard Estep:
Interview with
Brittney Isley & Stephen Erkintalo

Brittney Isley is founder/investigator of the group Spiritual Encounters. Her colleague, Stephen Erkintalo, is a paranormal investigator.

Brittney was with a paranormal events company when she first went to Farrar Elementary in the summer of 2018. It was an experience that she would never forget.

"It only took one visit, and I was hooked," she laughs. She, in turn, introduced fellow investigator Stephen to the school. He would end up filming a documentary about Farrar.

"I knew as soon as I stepped foot on the grounds that this was not the same as the other locations I had been to," Brittney begins, echoing the words of many other people that we have spoken to about Farrar. "The locker doors were slamming throughout the night. We heard a lot of noises that were difficult to explain, especially the disembodied giggling. The sound of footsteps walking around in empty rooms."

In a spectacular turn of events, a water jug was hurled through the air at Brittney, missing her by just a split-second, and instead hitting the boiler room door, which she had just closed behind her.

This tracks with Seth Alne's opinion that the paranormal activity down in the boiler room is getting darker and more negative in nature — after all, what clearer indication could there have been that something wanted Brittney to get out of there than throwing something at her?

This remarkable incident happened in the presence of multiple eyewitnesses, all guests on a public event that she was helping to run. Brittney had just led them into the boiler room and pulled the door shut when it happened. Several of the visiting guests were clearly terrified at what had just taken place, whereas others were excited to see that Farrar Elementary was living up to its reputation already.

"As somebody who is able to connect with spirit, a lot of my experiences are difficult to prove. They're very subjective," she cautions me as the interview starts moving forward.

"We went to film the documentary there just a few days before Christmas," Stephen interjects. "And we all had our own different experiences during that visit."

I ask him to give some examples.

"In the auditorium, we performed a ritual to 'open up the veil,'" he responds. Whether one believes that such spells and ceremonies actually work is for the reader to decide, but it is fascinating to note that while nobody noticed it at the time, the team seems to have attracted a very special guest. It was only upon reviewing the video footage of the incident afterward that they saw a dark figure had appeared on the stage behind them.

They also heard the sound of a woman's voice singing, coming from the upper floors — could this have been the same disembodied female voice that had called down to us from the second floor, the spirit that we are assuming could be the Librarian?

Voices, bangs, and other audio phenomena accompanied Brittney and Stephen throughout the night. Most of it seemed to be centered around the auditorium, which got progressively louder once the team had relocated to the second floor. There seemed to be a game of cat and mouse going on.

"We caught a *big* shadow figure on video," Brittney goes on, "running right past the camera. That impressed the heck out of us both."

One strange thing is that despite her having visited Farrar four times, she has never experienced anything paranormal in the vicinity of the principal's office. Many visitors find that to be a — if not *the*— hotspot, but Brittney has always found that area to be inert.

I ask her about the Principal, and the other entities that haunt Farrar. She tells me that she senses a large (eight feet tall) shadowy entity that hangs out up on the third floor, near the principal's office… one that is most definitely not human. "That's just my perception," she is quick to point out, "and I can't say that this is the same entity people are referring to as the Principal. But it's up there, and it's not nice."

While Brittney is not overly fond of the boiler room, the part of Farrar that Stephen dislikes the most are the bathrooms, situated downstairs in the gymnasium. "I just don't like the way it feels down there," he says. "It makes me feel uneasy in there... in fact, those bathrooms terrified me, *and* the rest of my team. We didn't even document anything in there, but none of our group would go in there alone."

"The break room scares me the most," Brittney says, referring to the room which Stephen, Erik and I used for our headquarters, thanks to the comfortable furniture, microwave, and fridge it provided... not to mention the temperature control.

"Why is that?" I ask, intrigued because I had never even considered the possibility that the break room might be haunted.

The atmosphere in there had never felt anything other than warm and friendly to me during our stay at Farrar.

"Think about the fact that most teams use that room for charging their equipment and reviewing evidence," Stephen interjects. "That's a lot of free potential energy for the spirits to make use of. I believe that when we review our evidence there in that room, we release our own energy in there, especially when we get excited over what it is that we're capturing."

If Stephen is right, then a big piece of the Farrar puzzle was sitting right under our nose all along, because none of us had thought to investigate that room. There hadn't been any stories or claims of paranormal activity associated with it, as far as we knew at the time.

(Note to future Farrar investigators: spend some time checking out the break room).

The topic of conversation turns toward the children of Farrar. Are these genuinely the spirits of children, I ask, or something that is simply masquerading as such... or a mixture of both?

"I have interacted with child spirits there," Brittney maintains. "But I've also encountered things that are simply *pretending* to be spirits. I'll never forget what was supposedly a little boy. I made contact with it in the closet of Mrs. Martin's classroom. It was most definitely *not* a child — I saw it for what it *really* was."

"Which was what?" I ask, suspecting that I know the answer already.

This entity was dark, and Brittney claims to have seen it to be releasing crawlers into the room. ('Crawlers' is a term she uses to describe the small minion spirits of negative entities). The so-called 'boy' refused to talk to Brittney, but was unable to prevent her from seeing its true face.

Why do Brittney and Stephen believe that Farrar is haunted? Brittney answers first.

"For me, it's all about the land, and the Native Americans that once lived there," she says.

Stephen tends to agree. "The sheer amount of energy on that land is just *phenomenal*. So many types of different activities and rituals could have been carried out there before the school was even built."

If they are both correct, then the key to the haunting of Farrar Elementary was forged long before the first brick was ever laid in the school foundation.

Chapter Fifteen
Richard Estep:
Interview with David Rountree
(written by E. E. Bensen)

In listening to an hour-long recording of an interview done by Richard, I can certainly say that David Rountree is an interesting guy.

While the conversation went off the Farrar topic many times, it never ceased to be interesting in its own right for sure. David has certainly spent countless hours thinking about the paranormal from an angle that many people never do.

When it comes to Farrar, and the question of why it might be haunted, he feels that it is primarily due to the land it is sitting on, as expressed by other contributors to this book. Additionally, he was quick to point out that it has no dark history to speak of. As we've discussed, the *Ghost*

Stalkers TV show focused on the concept of portals, or as David prefers to call them, wormholes. While only a small portion of the actual results of his experiments were touched upon in the show, he listed off a series of data points that he collected at Farrar when the team believed paranormal activity was happening. These include a localized alteration of environment, such as: inconsistent atmospheric pressure, temperature variance, fluctuations in air conductivity, and an altered flow of time.

On the last point, David did go into some detail as to how he constructed a device to measure time data having to do with multiple chronograph-type instruments; however, I'll admit that my computer science background is insufficient to do it much justice here, so I won't embarrass myself trying, but my logical brain was fine with the explanation for what it's worth. He believes that the data collected is evidence of the portals the show focused on.

During the *Ghost Stalkers* episode, David used various health monitoring devices on both Chad and John, such as an EEG meter, and blood pressure and heart rate monitors. Both Richard and I were pleased that he was keen to point out that simply being in the building was clearly bothering Chad and resulting in elevated readings, and that it wasn't necessarily related to anything remotely paranormal. As researchers, we have to refrain from immediately jumping to any conclusions.

Over the course of the interview, David indicated that he believes paranormal activity occurs when there is a human catalyst and the energy fields of the living clash with those of whatever it is that we're experiencing. In other words, no people equals no paranormal activity. This is one area that I actually have to question, based solely on my own research over the years.

While I do think that people can be a catalyst at times, I've collected many recordings in completely empty locations that have ranged from objects moving (including my voice recorder), audible voices referring to the equipment, random singing, phantom conversations, doors being opened or closed, and the list goes on and on. Perhaps we can settle on a happy medium and agree that while absent from the location, our *intent* was still floating out there in the ether somehow, thanks to the investigative equipment that we left behind.

During the filming of the show, David pointed out that most of the activity in the building seemed to be centered on the third floor near the principal's office and in the auditorium. This is certainly consistent with many of the reports we've already discussed here, as well as with my own experiences in the building. He placed six seismic sensors in the auditorium, and the team observed movement in the area by something unseen. The sensors were unable to be triggered by even walking down the hallway nearby.

David also pointed out that while using a smoke machine for quite some time, then allowing the resultant haze to settle for a few minutes, a swirling vortex appeared in front of Chad, who reported that he was afraid to breathe as he watched it form. This unfortunately ended up on the cutting room floor and never made the show, but there was no physical reason found for it to have happened in the first place. I can't help but to again be reminded of the strange visual effect that Stephen and I experienced in the auditorium at Farrar.

As for the bizarre voice recorder behavior experienced by John Tenney, David believes that something must have been disrupting the electronics in the device, and he insists that it would be some sort of RF frequency.

And what of the shadow figures witnessed by many in the school? David believes them to be humanoid-like beings of unknown origin based on anti-photonic radiation. Some research has indicated that our very DNA can fluoresce and emit ultraviolet photons, or light, in simple terms. If these shadow figures were comprised of the opposite, they would, theoretically, *absorb* light.

In my first book, I described the experience of shining my flashlight on the shadow figure at Farrar by saying, "The light seemed absorbed by it, rather than reflecting off of it in any way." Perhaps there is something to my rather innocent and admittedly nowhere-near-scientific observation? David went on to say that he observed a shadow figure recoil away from the beam of a laser grid device in the Springfield State Hospital episode, as though it was painful to it.

As for our experiences at Farrar, Richard described the fantastic disembodied voice response we got from the second floor, returning his friendly "Hello". It is David's assertion that such voices represent a mechanical form of energy, meaning that enough matter and mass must have been materialized to create the sound vibration we heard with our ears. That certainly seems logical, although I'd add that if true, whatever is manifesting doesn't always have to be visible as well. I've had very loud disembodied voices occur right in front of my face, and I didn't actually *see* anything at all. I physically *felt* the sound vibration from a very long moan that manifested only feet away from us in the Washoe Club a few years ago. There was certainly nothing visible in that case either, because if there had been, I'd be long since dead from a heart attack. That scared the absolute hell out of me.

Richard went on to describe Stephen's rather puzzling experience of hearing a loud scream while neither of the two of us heard anything at all. Acoustically speaking, this is completely impossible in the schoolhouse. David's take on this was that the most likely explanation goes back to the portal theory. He asserted that a portal may manifest in only a very small space, such as 2 to 3 meters. Therefore, Stephen just so happened to be in the middle of it. Richard and I wouldn't have heard the sound, because it quite literally didn't exist within our respective physical spaces and dimension. Did I mention that David Rountree is an interesting guy? This gives me quite a bit of food for thought, because I can't tell you how many times I've been on investigations when only one person present hears something that should have been clearly audible to everyone.

Could this portal theory be at least one of the root causes of this?

Unsurprisingly, at the end of the interview, David was

able to leave us with one last thought-provoking tidbit. One of the most common voice recordings in the field of paranormal research is to capture the words, "Get Out!" I would venture to say that based on my experience in the field, and the numerous investigators I've talked with over the years, that just about everyone records one of these eventually. It has almost become a joke, because of just how common that message is to receive.

Naturally, the most obvious assumption is that whatever entities we are engaging with simply want to be left alone, and want us humans to vacate their space. We assume that they perceive us as intruders and want us out. Of course, if you're David Rountree, the most obvious assumption is something else entirely.

What if these strange and unexplained voices telling us to "get out" are actually trying to *save* us from something? And if so, from *what*?

Chapter Sixteen

E. E. Bensen:
Interview with Nancy Oliver

I had the great privilege of chatting with Nancy Oliver over the phone for about 30 minutes recently. She and her husband Jim own the Farrar schoolhouse, and really are the driving force behind why it is open to investigators today.

The reason for them buying the building actually had nothing whatsoever to do with the paranormal. The plan originally was to fix it up and offer it as a venue for weddings, and meetings, and whatnot. While that has never come to pass, the reason that they still own the building today, is directly related the revenue generated by paranormal investigations. Nancy was quick to point out that they nearly lost the building due to financial concerns; however, they have since been able to maintain the aging structure and continue using it as a home to the present day.

The genesis of paranormal investigations taking place at Farrar goes back to 2007, when psychic Jacqui Carpenter randomly showed up in the driveway of the school, and informed Nancy that there was the spirit of a little girl in the building. This only served to confirm suspicions that Nancy and Jim had already formed about the school, and their strange experiences within its walls since purchasing the place about a year prior in 2006.

The first investigation of the building then took place, during which the very first EVP captured at the school was collected in the second-floor boys' bathroom. A voice was picked up on video camera audio saying, "She's in the bathroom." This certainly goes a long way to debunking some skeptic's assertions that EVP is simply rogue radio waves or shortwave radio interference somehow picked up by the recording device (something which I have never encountered myself in countless hours of reviewing recordings I'll add).

Sadly, Jacqui is no longer with us as of June 2014, but her impact on all those who have come after her and explored the school is significant. When I trace back the origin of me catching that shadow figure in my flashlight beam, and seeing one of the coolest things I've ever witnessed in my life, I have to give a nod to Jacqui for her part in making that possible. Thanks, Jacqui.

Nancy went on to describe one of her most impressive experiences that happened very early on after buying the building. She was in the gymnasium at around eleven o'clock in the morning, and headed for the stairs leading up to the next floor. Upon rounding the corner to the stairway, she saw a little boy standing on the stairs, one foot on the bottom step, and one hand on the railing. He was about four feet tall, and was not transparent at all, yet gray in color and fuzzy around the edges. The boy vanished, leaving Nancy to contemplate what she had just seen. Nancy was also quick to point out that the lights were on, in addition to the natural light entering the building. I love hearing about paranormal experiences such as this. It is quite satisfying when something happens that is utterly unable to be explained away.

As haunted as the schoolhouse is, and the fact that Jim and Nancy actually have private living quarters on the main floor, I asked the obvious question of whether they experience any paranormal activity in their space. She indicated that they generally do not, which I found interesting. It would seem that whatever haunts Farrar is respectful of their space. She did mention that occasionally on the floors above them, they will hear what sounds like someone or something falling over, or what sounds like metal being dragged across the floor. They have never been able to identify where those sounds come from.

Lastly, Nancy wanted to point out that she is so very thankful for all the folks that visit the school respectfully, and help to keep the lights on. I was glad to hear that they have seldom had any real problems with people doing stupid things or tearing the place up. After all, that just ruins it for the rest of us.

As for Nancy and Jim, I would like to send a heartfelt 'thank you' right back at them for letting us spend time in the place. I think I can safely speak for the paranormal community as a whole, when I say that it truly is *our privilege.*

Afterword
E. E. Bensen

The Farrar school is a bit of an anomaly when considering the array of places that fall within the "known haunted" list. It has no extensive dark history that I am aware of.

There is also no body count. Instead, what we have is a relatively unassuming building situated amongst the farm fields in rural Iowa, that also happens to be one of the most haunted places I've ever had the good fortune to be able to explore.

Time and again, it has delivered some of the most profound paranormal experiences that I've ever had while travelling the country and spending countless hours in the dark.

I have no real explanation for why Farrar would be as haunted as it is. Truthfully, this mystery is exactly what draws me to it. Perhaps it is the land upon which it sits, and the spirits within the building that predate the structure by decades, centuries, or perhaps even millennia. Maybe the haunting is a result of some sort of strange space-time anomaly or portal, allowing the realities of our dimension and others to collide in that space. It is also plausible that repeated investigation of the building is serving to now amplify the haunting and to bring in other entities of some unknown origin.

Perhaps what started as mere curiosity and a couple of campfire ghost stories about a haunted school has now turned into some seriously high levels of paranormal activity. The possible theories are numerous to be sure, and I have little hope that we'll ever have a definitive answer in my lifetime.

What I *can* say, with reasonable certainty, is that whatever or whoever is haunting Farrar is surely of an intelligent nature. It is not uncommon to encounter hauntings in the field of paranormal research that are considered to be of a residual nature. In these cases, the phenomena, in whatever form it may be whether auditory, olfactory, or visual, seems to occur regardless of who may be present at the time. It is much like a recording being played back over and over on some sort of ethereal endless loop. While I can say that this type of haunting is indeed fascinating in its own right, I'll also say that in terms of paranormal research it's the equivalent of a booby prize to most investigators. Intelligent hauntings are significantly more interesting for obvious reasons, especially for those of us who have had eventful experiences in the field.

The shadowy figures that I have encountered at Farrar on multiple occasions were most certainly not just going about their business and totally oblivious to me. Clearly, they were every bit as interested in me as I was in them. This is both a thrilling and admittedly somewhat disconcerting thought. Apparently, physical boundaries mean little or nothing to them, and my mind always drifts to thoughts of where they might be right now. Who can say whether they are confined to the space that is currently that rural schoolhouse, or whether they can go anywhere they might wish to be?

Who can really say whether one of them is watching me, or you, right now? As I sit at my desk late at night in a quiet house, I will admit to you that my eyes just lingered on the open door and deep down I wished that I had left the light on in the hall.

The paranormal has been a lifelong interest of mine. I set out many years ago trying to answer the big questions that nearly everyone asks such as, "Is there an afterlife?" and "What happens when we die?" My journey in the field has taken me to places far from home, and put me into situations that I never thought I would be in (on purpose, no less).

Simply watching television investigations and hearing word of mouth stories from others certainly can be exciting; however there really is no substitute for standing alone in the dark and witnessing paranormal events for yourself when you suddenly notice that the other members of your team are not particularly close by. For me as an investigator, this is truly the essence of the search for the unknown, and there is nothing else quite like it.

It is often an exercise in being fascinated, excited, and terrified all in the same exhilarating moment.

The Farrar school has provided me with multiple experiences like that over the past few years, and I am so very thankful to have had them. It is hard to translate the feeling into words of standing face-to-face with the infamous shadow figure on the top floor, my flashlight beam illuminating everything around it, and locked in a mutual gaze. I was witnessing something that should not be possible, yet, there it was: an utter aberration of conventional wisdom and science looking back at me.

I've somehow always known deep down that these things exist, however standing there in the dark and staring it directly in the "face" is still quite sobering. Thanks to the schoolhouse, and whatever that thing is, I will take the image to the grave as it is forever burned into my memory. I can't un-see it, and honestly, I don't want to.

I would encourage you, the reader, to consider exploring those mysteries for yourself sometime. If you do visit, please don't think of the place as "abandoned" since it most surely is not. It is occupied by not only the living, who care for the building, but also by something incredible and not of our physical realm. It is one of my favorite places to investigate, so please, treat it kindly so that it may be preserved for others in the future.

Lastly, Richard and I just want to thank you for taking an interest in our little paranormal adventure, and in the mystery that is the haunting at Farrar…

Thanks

The authors would like to thank: Nancy & Jim Oliver for
opening the doors of Farrar Elementary to the public;
Stephen Weidner, for joining us on our expedition;
Will & Jacquelyn Conkel, and Jonah Jones for giving us the
grand tour;
all of our interviewees, for kindly sharing their personal
experiences;
… and last, but by no means least, John Tenney for
contributing to this project in a big way.

About the Authors

Richard Estep is a paramedic and paranormal investigator who hails from Great Britain, and currently makes his home in the United States. His work features on the TV series "Haunted Case Files," "Haunted Hospitals," and "Paranormal 911." When he's not traveling the world collecting ghost stories and investigating haunted houses, he is writing about those very same places, or having fun writing fiction with a distinctly supernatural theme to it. Visit his website at: www.richardestep.net.

E. E. Bensen is a reluctant independent author, an IT professional, avid motorcyclist, gamer, bowler, guitar player, nerd, and is sometimes said to have a questionable sense of humor. He lives in Colorado.

Other Books by Richard Estep

Haunted Healthcare

Haunted Healthcare 2

The World's Most Haunted Hospitals

The Haunting of Asylum 49

Haunted Longmont

The Dead Below: The Haunting of Denver Botanic Gardens

The Horrors of Fox Hollow Farm

The Devil's Coming to Get Me: The Haunting of Malvern Manor

The Fairfield Haunting: On the Gettysburg Ghost Trail

The Farnsworth House Haunting: On the Gettysburg Ghost Trail

In Search of the Paranormal

Trail of Terror

Colorado UFOs

Visiting the Ghost Ward

Other Books by E. E. Bensen

Supposedly Haunted: True Life Experiences of a Paranormal Investigator

Of Ghostly Origins: More True Life Experiences of a Paranormal Investigator

Printed in Great Britain
by Amazon

45098929R00172